GROWING IN grace WITH GRACE

GRACE M. BLUE

Copyright © 2020 Grace M. Blue

Unless otherwise indicated, all Scripture quotations are taken from the Holy Bible, New Living Translation, copyright © 1996, 2004, 2015 by Tyndale House Foundation. Used by permission of Tyndale House Publishers, Inc., Carol Stream, Illinois 60188. All rights reserved. "Scripture quotations are from the ESV® Bible (The Holy Bible, English Standard Version®), copyright © 2001 by Crossway, a publishing ministry of Good News Publishers. Used by permission. All rights reserved." Scripture quotations from The Authorized (King James) Version. Rights in the Authorized Version in the United Kingdom are vested in the Crown. Reproduced by permission of the Crown's patentee, Cambridge University Press

All rights reserved. No part of this document may be reproduced or transmitted in any form or by any means, electronic, mechanical, photocopying, recording, or otherwise, without prior written permission of the author.

GROWING IN GRACE
With Grace

Grace M. Blue
C/O Cincinnati Bible Way Church
5103 Chapman Ave., Cincinnati, Ohio 45227
(513) 561-7764, graceblue@me.com

Illustrations used with Permission by Ian Coate
https://www.freechristianillustrations.com/about.html

ISBN: 978-1-949826-27-2
Printed in the USA.
All rights reserved

Published by: EAGLES GLOBAL BOOKS | Frisco, Texas
In conjunction with the 2020 Eagles Authors Course
Cover & interior designed by DestinedToPublish.com | (773) 783-2981

ACKNOWLEDGMENTS

First and foremost, all glory and thanks go to my Father God and my Lord and Saviour Jesus Christ, who gave me the strength, courage, and wisdom that I needed to bring this project from my heart to my hands.

To my wonderful loving husband, Apostle James E. Blue Jr., who has always encouraged and brought out the best in me, and who pushed and pulled me to the completion of this project. I love me some him!!

To my late mother, Ruby M. Gray, who was such a great example of a woman who loved the Lord and people, whose brightness pierced the darkness, and who encouraged me in all that I did. To my late dad, Charles L. Gray, who raised me as his own daughter and exposed me to books and educational experiences that I could've only imagined. And to my wonderful, generous mother-in-love, the late Verilla V. Blue, a powerful loving minister of the gospel who was such a great example of an overcomer!

To my courageous, powerful, visionary, anointed mother in the Lord, Bishop Patricia T. Whitelocke, who was so instrumental in my spiritual growth and always saw the best in me and countless others, and so lovingly pulled the best out of me.

To our children, Patricia, Brian Sr., Angelene, Eugene, James III, and Grace Victoria, and our grandchildren, Karizma, Brian Jr., Braylon, Brandon, Zaria Grace, Jordyn, Brycen, Jameson, Gracelynn, and Braxton, you are my love and joy!! A special thanks to my daughters, who encouraged me and assisted me financially to make sure I had no excuses in finishing this project.

To all the people of God I've had the privilege and honor to pastor and/or speak into your lives, thank you. Even with the mistakes I made, many of you were gracious enough to forgive me, love me, and allow me room to grow. A very big loving thanks to our Cincinnati Bible Way Church family for allowing Apostle James and me to pastor such a great body of Believers. We both love you so much and thank God for your love and support.

A final thanks to Ian and Sue Coate from Australia, who allowed me to use their Free Christian Illustrations in my book. Many blessings to you both!

FOREWORD

I encouraged Apostle Grace, as she often encourages me, to pursue one of her heart assignments. This book is the result of this. When you read this book, please give the Holy Spirit liberty to speak to you and demonstrate the many illustrations presented. As Apostle Grace shares her narrative, you will be challenged as a new believer, a seasoned believer, leader, teacher, or someone looking for permanent change and authentic growth. This book answers the questions "who's growing up, and why grow up?" and gives practical guidelines of how to do this.

I have known my wife, Grace Marie, to be an exceptional person whom I love and appreciate so much as her husband of 44 years, which equates to fifty years when including our six-year courtship. I have had the honor and privilege to live and work alongside her in marriage, raising our family, ministry, and many adventures in faith and life.

She wanted to write this book to speak to the challenges concerning the many people we have met and ministered to for over forty years in ministry together. Her concern was the spiritual growth of those we ministered to who remained the same after all those years and the encouragement of those who made the choice to spiritually mature.

This book is a tool to train and refresh our minds about who we are and how we should function as mature members of the Body of Christ. If you want to grow spiritually, this book is for you; if you want to help someone else grow spiritually, this book is for you. I highly recommend this work of love to help you raise the bar in your own life first and then help others.

Use this work as a study guide for true discipleship, or use it as a checklist for your leadership team and personal friends.

Together, Doing God's Word, His Will, His Way,

Apostle James E. Blue Jr.,
Senior Pastor
Cincinnati Bible Way Church

CONTENTS

Acknowledgments i

Foreword iii

Contents v

Introduction vii

Chapter 1:
Authentic Spiritual Growth 1

Chapter 2:
Who Are You In Christ Jesus, And What
Is Your Responsibility As A Believer? 11

    A. Standing vs. State 16
    B. Where Do You Stand? 18
    C. What State Are You In? "Location, Location, Location!" 25

Chapter 3:
Spiritual Maturity 29

    A. You Are Responsible! 33
    B. Movement vs. Stagnation 36
    C. If You Wanna Grow, Renew Your Mind! 40

Chapter 4:
Developmental Stages of The Sons Of God 52

    A. The "Gester" of God 62
    B. The "Nepios" of God 70
    C. The "Paidion" of God 81

Chapter 5:
Developmental Stages of Spiritual Growth **90**

    D. The "Pais" of God 90
    E. The "Teknon" of God 96
    F. The "Neaniskos" of God 102
    G. The "Huios" of God 105

Chapter 6:
Our Help Comes From The Lord – The Five Graces **111**

    A. The Holy Spirit 116
    B. The Holy Bible 127
    C. The Five-Fold Ministry 134
    D. Progenitors 140
    E. His Amazing Grace 146

Chapter 7:
Our Help Comes From The Lord – The Five Graces **153**

Takeaways **157**

Bibliography **161**

INTRODUCTION

"But grow in the grace and knowledge of our Lord and Savior Jesus Christ. To him be glory both now and forever! Amen."
(2 Peter 3:18 NIV)

There is a saying, "Many Christians grow up in church, but never grow in Christ. They know hymns but don't know Him."

As a believer in Jesus Christ, have you felt that although you were singing in the choir, laying hands on the sick, attending conference after conference, reading how-to Christian books, watching Christian TV, following charismatic leaders, and believing you were obedient to leadership, something was still missing? How many are looking for signs, miracles, and wonders: the works that

Jesus did and said we could do the same but even greater because He was going to His Father in heaven?

I wrote this book because I believe that we as believers in our Lord and Saviour JESUS CHRIST are looking for more. We are wanting more from this spirituality. As a Pastor for over 35 years, I have noted that no matter how much Sunday preaching and Bible Study some people attended, they were still the same way they had been before, after years of being in the Word of God. They were frustrated, and we as Pastors were frustrated too. I realized that believers were not truthfully looking at themselves to determine that changes and growth needed to be made in the life of the believer. I also realized that some believers didn't know how to do that. I have found the importance of examining ourselves to make sure we are authentically growing in God's grace and with God's grace. I have also found that too many believers in Christ Jesus are satisfied with just being saved but not living the saved life. Too many believers don't realize that fully living the abundant life that Jesus promised in John 10:10 really requires a renewed mind because the old mindset, the sinful mind, the "me, myself, and I" mindset gets in the way of really experiencing God and knowing what He has available, how to receive it, and how to give Him glory in it.

I've been thinking about a term that's often thrown around to describe what a church is supposed to be. They say a church is a hospital where believers come to get healed and made whole. I agreed with that until I started thinking more about it and came to the conclusion that if the church is a hospital, then those who come just to get cured or healed will leave, like they do a hospital, and

INTRODUCTION

never come back nor want to come back. I know if I'm a patient in a hospital, and my ailment is cured and I go home, my intention is not to come back to the hospital, because I associate those who are in the hospital with having sickness and disease and going there to get it healed.

The church isn't a hospital. Yes, you do go to the House of the Lord to receive healing and wholeness, but that's not all you receive there. The church, as my husband James says, is a vehicle to lead you to the fullness of the Kingdom of God and its righteousness. I also equate the church with being a place that we go to get our marching orders, like the military. It is a place where Believers in Jesus Christ come together and worship God in the beauty of His holiness. It is a place where functioning members come to learn to give of themselves, and to learn their gifting and their calling and how to walk in them. It's a place where we come and exercise the unity of the Spirit with each other of one accord, in one place, worshiping God and expecting Him to move in mighty, miraculous ways. It is a place where a Believer learns to grow in the grace of God, knowing our Saviour and becoming more and more like Him.

During my Christian walk and in my time as a Pastor, I've noted that many of our young people grow up in the church and in many cases are made to go to church. But when they reach the age of biological maturity, they leave the church and don't come back. Why is that? Why is it that we are seeing the same sins in the church as we see in the world, but so few are addressing those sin issues? Why is it that we are lacking in the love that Jesus walked in to the point of forgiving those who crucified Him? Why is it that we are seeing believers behaving more like the world than like Jesus?

We are living in a time when many believers in Jesus Christ are disillusioned because they don't experience the changes in their lives that are promised as a result of coming to Christ. Unfortunately, in many believers' eyes, the focus is on "what has God done for me lately?" and on gaining material wealth instead of the wealth of knowing Him. In my own personal spiritual journey, I have realized that there is a fulfillment in my mind, my body, my soul, and my spirit that is so satisfying and regenerating. It comes from knowing Jesus and having the right type of relationship and understanding of who He meant me to be in Him.

But there is more to knowing Him than just His acts or what He does and can do for me. I've seen too many people focus on what He's done or doing for them rather than on knowing His ways. Knowing Him! As I grew to know Him, I began to let my own wants and needs take a back seat, and to put Him in the front seat and focus on what He needed from me. But that didn't happen overnight for me. I had to mature to get to that point. When I first came to Christ, I was born again, and just like in a natural birth, I had to go through the process of growing and maturing. But I had to learn to grow authentically. It's not how long you've been a Christian that makes you mature but how you allow the Christ in you to occupy the seat of your mind, will, and emotions.

What does it mean to be authentic in your spiritual growing process? Well, a weed grows, but in many cases, a weed doesn't really have a positive purpose. I look at the weed as being more selfish because

INTRODUCTION

as it grows, it chokes out the plant growing next to it that's needed by humanity and the environment to thrive. Being authentic comes from within. It means our beliefs and values coincide and conform with our actions and words. It's being our real selves. What I'm doing and saying is equivalent to what I believe, think, and feel. I'm not saying with my mouth that I love my church member while harboring anger and strife against them inside of me. That's what's called being hypocritical. In too many cases like this, we're missing authentic spiritual growth in the land of Christendom, Saints!

So, how do I grow authentically and not be a hypocrite? That's what I want to address in this book.

I believe that after reading this book, you will be excited and determined to say, "I'm going to take this walk in Christ seriously and purposefully and have authentic spiritual growth, because my life and the lives of others I touch depend upon it." So, Let's Grow Deep and Grow Up in Him!

CHAPTER 1:
AUTHENTIC SPIRITUAL GROWTH

We have too many believers that are Baby Hueys, Skunks in the Pews, Pigs in the Pen, Butts in the Seats, and Busy Beavers. Have you ever wondered about all these characters that might be part of a church's congregation? Well, I have!

I've been a Christian for most of my life and in ministry for over 35 years, and I've seen a lot of faces, been to a lot of places, and have wondered why people who receive salvation and profess their love for God stay the same way they were before they came to Christ. They claim that they've changed or don't care that they need to change and get better, but their life is not a reflection of the Christ inside. Too many believers, once they come to Christ, believe they've arrived. Yes, Praise God, we've arrived into the Kingdom of God! But now that we've arrived, it's the beginning of understanding our true identity in Christ and learning how to be true citizens of the Kingdom of God.

Back in the 1950s, there was a cartoon character named Baby Huey. Baby Huey was an overgrown duck with a baby-like vocabulary and grammar. Everything he did and said sounded like he was between the ages of three and six years old. He never grew up to become the productive adult duck he was destined to be. Too many Christians never allow themselves to become spiritually mature. They never develop any further than when they first came to Christ, and as a result, they are never able to live in their purpose and complete their God-given assignment.

Anyone who has been sprayed by a skunk or experienced the skunk smell knows it is unbearable. Well, sometimes in church congregations, you may have Skunks in the Pews. You may think that I'm talking about literal skunks, but I'm talking about people who smell bad in the Spirit because of their attitude or actions. Just like a literal skunk, they stink up everyone around them with a stench that's hard to get off. A skunk smell, once it gets on you, contaminates you with that terrible odor, and no one wants to be around you. They avoid you like the plague. A Skunk in the Pew may come in the guise of someone constantly criticizing and complaining about the leadership, about the facilities, about their life: you name it, they're complaining about it. It can also come in the form of unforgiveness, anger, and strife. A literal skunk also releases their smell if they feel they're in danger. This is how you can tell someone is a Skunk in the Pew: they won't do anything to get better by neutralizing their smell. If you get too close to them, to try to correct them or help them, they emit their stinky spray towards you and the stench will be upon you! What a skunk does contaminates you. The contamination could be in the form of the sin they repeatedly commit, the attitude they invoke, or even the negative rhetoric they release on others.

> *"Beloved ones, with promises like these, and because of our deepest respect and worship of God, we must remove everything from our lives that contaminates body and spirit, and continue to complete the development of holiness within us." (2 Corinthians 7:1 TPT)*

Let's talk about those Pigs in the Pen and how they are related to stunted growth in His grace. Keep in mind that pigs have exceptional hearing and smell but very poor eyesight, and they'll eat almost anything, including human bones. If you have Pigs in the Pen (Pew), they'll hear the Word of God but not see how it pertains or relates to them. In fact, they will look for other things to feed themselves on that may not be conducive to their spiritual growth and development, nor to the spiritual growth and development of others. Many times it can be destructive. They may gravitate towards witchcraft and try to mix it with Christianity.

> *"But if you continue to criticize and come against each other over minor issues, you're acting like wild beasts trying to destroy one another!" (Galatians 5:15 TPT)*

What about those wild Dogs in the Hall? These are not your ordinary trusting, playful, dependable, friendly canine. They never really come into the sanctuary, but spend their time on the outward perimeter, barking and complaining about how church should be and what it ought to be. The wild Dogs in the Hall have not fully committed themselves to life according to the Word of God nor to the people of God; instead, their delight is to cause havoc in the life of the church. The wild Dogs in the Hall have not fully come into the sanctuary to dwell in the knowledge of God and have a relationship with Him. Their barks and growls are directed to divert other believers from going into the sanctuary to enter into His presence and receive His goodness.

Butts in the Seats is all they are and seemingly ever want to be. The believers of Jesus Christ who fit in this category just want to come to church and listen to the Word of God and leave, not transformed by the betterment of their hearts and minds, but content to remain the same. In fact, they may even profess a love of God and their fellow man, but still, their butts are just in their seats. Their motivation in coming to church may be just because it's required, or because they grew up in the church, or because they can hobnob with influential people who attend that church, or it makes them look holy, or a combination of all of the above. But for whatever reason, their intention is not to renew their minds.

> *"Don't just listen to the Word of Truth and not respond to it, for that is the essence of self-deception. So always let his Word become like poetry written and fulfilled by your life!" (James 1:22 TPT)*

Butts in the Seats, as my husband both humorously and seriously says, may also be the first and third Sunday or second and fourth Sunday Christians. They don't come to church consistently enough to learn the Word of God in order to live a transformed life. In fact, they want church to be over quickly so they can go do other things that are seemingly more pleasurable. As I have said many times, give God something to work with.

> *"This is not the time to pull away and neglect meeting together, as some have formed the habit of doing, because we need each other! In fact, we should come together even more frequently, eager to encourage and urge each other onward as we anticipate that day dawning."* (Hebrews 10:25 TPT)

What about the Busy Beavers? They're so busy doing church business that they have no time to deal with spiritual growth nor to be in intimate communion with the Lord. Their focus has been on singing in the choir, serving in the church, serving on the board. In fact, sometimes the Busy Beavers think busyness equates to being closer to God. In the Bible, that's what Martha thought. She was so busy with the preparation for Jesus coming that when He came, she made no time for Him. She made no time to sit at His feet and be in His presence. On the contrary, her sister Mary sat at Jesus' feet to listen to Him break the Bread of Life through teachings she had never heard before. Mary knew the importance of being in His presence. Martha got so upset with Mary that she went to Jesus to complain (Luke 10:38-42). But Jesus told her that Mary made the better choice. It looks good to be busy, but it's better to be in His presence.

Too many believers sit down and never make the progression that God intended for them to make, to move from New Believers to Manifested Sons and Daughters, those who come to full maturity in Christ Jesus. But then there are believers who understand and know the importance of spiritual growth and the necessity for change in their lives, according to Romans 12:1, but feel that it's all in vain because they're getting such backlash from the world or from immature Believers. If we're going to be all that God called and intended for us to be, by pressing toward that mark of the high calling in Christ Jesus, we must move to the original intent of God, to walk with Him and to have an intimate relationship with Him.

A spiritually immature person can do a lot of damage to themselves and to other people, especially if they are in leadership. For example, I've observed and experienced leaders who are very gifted and anointed with their gifting, and the call of God on their life is authentic, but because other leaders see their anointing, they want to advance them ahead of God's schedule and plan for them. Over the years I've noted and witnessed Pastors who are very charismatic in their preaching and in how they interact with people, but they have a flaw in their character that has to do with sexual sin. Because they are so charismatic, those who put them in positions of Pastoral leadership knew of their shortcomings but instead of mentoring them, confronting that flaw, and allowing God to tell them when they are ready, they push them into position. As a result, when their true character comes out in the open, they end up destroying lives and churches. Saints, it ought not be! As the old saying goes, they need to stay in the pews to be taught and challenged to mature instead of leading in the pulpit. There is a better way and a lasting way!

I've been a part of deliverance ministry for many years, and what a mighty ministry it is. It's believed that Jesus spent one-third of His time preaching, one-third healing, and one-third delivering people from the demonic. During a deliverance service, I've seen people writhing on the floor, yelling, screaming, and finally feeling a sense of freedom from demonic oppression. I've seen people truly set free and beginning to embrace the renewed mind walk, and I've also witnessed people who have been set free through the delivering power of Jesus Christ go back to the same habits and situations that got them there in the first place. Why do we see some who embrace the delivering power of Jesus and go on and live the more abundant life that Jesus promised in John 10:10, and then we see others who embrace the delivering power of Jesus but don't renew their mind, return back into the mess they were in, and miss living the more abundant life?

Even with water baptism, as my former pastor used to say, some go down in the water as dry devils and come out of the water as wet devils. There has to be a change!

When I stand before the judgment seat of Christ, I want to hear, "Well done!" Well done, because I fought a good fight and finished my course, my assignment. When I stand before Jesus, I want Him to see and then say to me that I was focused on being more like Him, and as I continued to grow spiritually, my roots were deep in Him. If my roots are deep in Him, then whatever dire circumstances or traumatic situations come my way, I won't easily be pulled up from my roots and toss my faith aside. If my roots are deep in Him, I am able to complete the assignment and purpose I was put on Planet Earth to do. I can't be a woman in little girl's shoes. My walk has to match my talk!

Unfortunately, ministry has become more performance based rather than worship based. Too many Believers in Christ come to church to be entertained, and church is looked upon as a place for entertainment, no different than going to a secular concert. We should go to the House of the Lord with the expectations of experiencing His presence as a collective body of Believers and listen to what He has to say, in order for us to be transformed by renewing our mind and to have impact as we go back out into the world.

In too many instances when one talks about church growth, it is viewed as a numbers game. How many physical bodies do we have in our church pews, and how many more can we get? The number one focus, unfortunately, has been on how to grow a church numerically, although much of what we call church growth, especially in the American church, comes from Believers moving from church to church, not from new converts growing in His grace and reproducing Kingdom-minded people. Don't get me wrong, we do want to see and participate in the expansion of God's Kingdom through new believers, and there are many, many books, articles, blogs, vlogs, and testimonies on how to grow your church numerically. But the Word of God speaks not only of making new disciples but of the spiritual growth of an individual believer. Jesus gave the commandment to the disciples before He ascended up into heaven.

> *"Then Jesus came close to them and said, 'All the authority of the universe has been given to me. Now go in my authority and make disciples of all nations, baptizing them in the name of the Father, the Son, and the Holy Spirit.* ***And teach them to faithfully follow all that I have commanded you. And never forget that I am with you every day, even to the completion of this age.'"***
> *(Matthew 28:18-20 TPT)*

John MacArthur notes that the word disciples is translated from the Greek word "mathetes," derived from "manthano," which "carries the connotation of intentional learning by inquiry and observation." It also generally means "one who engages in learning through instruction from another, *pupil, apprentice*." So, with that being noted, Jesus is not only saying to His disciples to go and make disciples but also telling them to remain disciples themselves. In other words, when we go and help others grow, we must remember that we are on the discipleship wheel too. It's not just for them, but it's for me to continue as a disciple of Jesus Christ.

In the days of megachurches, I remember when I was so concerned about our church growing numerically, and the Holy Spirit asked me, "Which is more important, quality or quantity? "I was wise enough to say, "Quality." When I speak of quality, I'm speaking of authentic quality of the believer's growth in Him. The focus on the individual growth of the believer has been switched to the numerical growth of a church, but being focused on the numbers of "butts in the seats" will keep us from focusing on "minds on the mission," which is an individual believer's authentic spiritual growth as they continue on the path of their God-given purpose and assignment.

Again, if we focus on quality, it's going to take maturity, because it takes time, effort, endurance, and perseverance to reap the harvest that builds and raises up multiple generations of impactful men and women of God who love God and take seriously their walk with Him and their divine purpose! There's a song we sang years ago that I believe sums it up: "A strong determination, a will to go all the way, faith in our God, to walk by our side, that's what it takes to run the race."

> *"And don't allow yourselves to be weary or disheartened in planting good seeds, for the season of reaping the wonderful harvest you've planted is coming!"* (Galatians 6:9 TPT)

MUSING: THOUGHTS TO PROVOKE

"It is a mistake to assess spirituality simply on the basis of a person's emotional display. What you want to be careful of is looking around at people in the church service and seeing people really into it – on their knees, people singing with glazed-over eyes, people expressing a lot of emotion, people weeping – and drawing the conclusion that because people are responding emotionally that they have a deeper connection with God or a more mature faith than the person who is not reacting emotionally at all. This is a profound error… Emotional response is not in any sense a Scriptural measure of spiritual maturity."
– Gregory Koukl

QUESTIONS TO PONDER:

What has bothered you about the growth of the believers you have observed? What has bothered you about your own growth as a believer in Jesus Christ?

CHAPTER 2:
WHO ARE YOU IN CHRIST JESUS, AND WHAT IS YOUR RESPONSIBILITY AS A BELIEVER?

A gift only becomes yours when you accept it.

So, who are we in Christ Jesus? What is our responsibility as Believers? I remember when a young girl, I was given the opportunity by my beloved Sunday School teacher to accept Jesus Christ as my Lord and Saviour. As I repeated the sinner's prayer, I received Jesus Christ in my heart. When I went home, I began to doubt and think that it was so easy to do, maybe there's more to being saved than what I did. So, I recited again about needing Jesus and knowing that I'm a sinner but I'm saved by His grace, mercy and love. I believe that Jesus is the Son of God, sent to save me from my sins. At such a young age, I still wasn't sure that I had done everything that I needed to do to be saved. I thought it had to be so much more. But as I continued to be taught the Word of God in Sunday School and church, I realized that I did do enough the first time I made the confession of faith in Jesus Christ, because

Jesus Did It All! Sometimes we feel that we have to do so much more than what God requires of us. But by His grace, through an act of my faith, I received the gift of eternal life.

Adam and Eve were created, formed, and made by God in His image, in His likeness, and He put them in a beautiful natural setting and told them to thrive. God had created an atmosphere of intimacy with Him so He could communicate with them and they could communicate with Him. God also gave them an assignment and told them of His original intent, which would help them thrive. He blessed them and told them in Genesis 1:28,

> "...Be **fruitful** and **multiply**; **fill** the earth and **subdue** it; have **dominion** over the fish of the sea, over the birds of the air, and over every living thing that moves on the earth." (NKJV)

God gave them dominion over the earth and in essence told them that it was their responsibility to make sure that the Kingdom of Heaven was revealed on earth. God created Adam and Eve to be the expression, representation, revelation, and connecting link between an invisible God and the visible creation. They were created to express, represent, and reveal God to His creation in such a way that it would be like heaven on earth. God's intent was that His will on earth would be the same as His will in heaven. Adam and Eve were to be God's representatives on an earthly plane to make sure that happened.

> "And the LORD God took the man, and put him in the garden of Eden to **dress** it and to **keep** it." (Genesis 2:15 KJV)

The Hebrew word *'abad,* **"to dress it,"** means "to work or serve" and refers to the ground or a garden. It can be defined as "to till or cultivate, to develop," that is, to be Fruitful, Multiply, and Replenish.

The Hebrew word *shamar,* **"to keep it,"** is a militaristic term meaning to keep, observe, preserve, beware, take heed, mark, regard, watch diligently, even spy, guarding something from the enemy – that is, to *Subdue* and take *Dominion.*

But an unnatural evil came to that perfect place, Eden, in the form of a serpent, Lucifer, and caused interference in Adam and Eve's relationship with the Father and the assignment He gave to them. Lucifer was after the hearts and minds of Adam and Eve. He wanted to separate their hearts and minds from the one who created and loved them, and turn their allegiance to themselves, which ultimately turned their allegiance to him, Lucifer. Lucifer asked one question: "Did God really say…?" That is the question our enemy Satan will always ask, because that question will always get us to question our relationship with God, what we believe He's said to us, and the assignment He gave to us. Adam and Eve fell for the lies of the enemy and rejected God, rebelling against Him and His plan for them to thrive and successfully reign and rule over the earth, thus putting a gap of separation between God and mankind because of sin. Adam and Eve never reached a level of maturity to carry out the instructions, the assignment that God gave them, which was to be fruitful, multiply, replenish, subdue, and take dominion. They were supposed to grab hold and understand the power and authority that God intended for them to walk in. But instead they allowed the lust of the flesh, the lust of the eyes, and the pride of life to have preeminence, and as a result fell into sin.

Even with what appeared to be a major setback of God's original intent, God had a plan to remove that interference and that gap of separation. That plan is called Jesus! Thank God for His plan! Even though Adam was the door for sin to come into the earth, Jesus was the door for heaven to come back to earth and redeem mankind from sin.

Because when the fullness of time came, God sent His Son, Jesus, born from a woman to remove the demonic interference and go back to God's original plan for mankind. That plan was for heaven to meet earth so that God's will in heaven would be on earth.

Jesus gave the final sacrifice for sin, restoring and reconciling mankind back into the family of God as the last Adam, according to 1 Corinthians 15:45,

> *"And so it is written, 'The first man Adam became a living being.' The last Adam became a life-giving spirit." (NKJV)*

> *"Under the old covenant, the priest stands and ministers before the altar day after day, offering the same sacrifices again and again, which can never take away sins. But our High Priest offered himself to God as a single sacrifice for sins, good for all time. Then he sat down in the place of honor at God's right hand." (Hebrews 10:11-12 NLT)*

> *"For God made Christ, who never sinned, to be the offering for our sin, so that we could be made right with God through Christ." (2 Corinthians 5:21 NLT)*

> *"For the grace of God has been revealed, bringing salvation to all people. And we are instructed to turn from godless living and sinful pleasures. We should live in this evil world with wisdom, righteousness, and devotion to God." (Titus 2:11-12 NLT)*

> *"Sin is no longer your master, for you no longer live under the requirements of the law. Instead, you live under the freedom of God's grace." (Romans 6:14 NLT)*

Jesus was tempted in every way by the devil, but He conquered sin by not giving in to sin like the first Adam did. Unlike Adam, Jesus attained a level of spiritual maturity that enabled Him to fulfill the purpose and assignment that His Father God had given Him. Jesus knew how to answer the devil when he tempted Jesus in the wilderness. He tried to use the same tactics he had used with Adam and Eve, but Jesus was wise enough to use God's exact words against the devil.

> *"He understands humanity, for as a Man, our magnificent King-Priest was tempted in every way just as we are, and conquered sin." (Hebrews 4:15 TPT)*

> *"He suffered and endured every test and temptation, so that he can help us every time we pass through the ordeals of life." (Hebrews 2:18 TPT)*

Our allegiance and devotion now is not to the world system nor to the Law of Moses, but to God as our Father because of His grace and mercy through the obedience and sacrifice of His Son and our Saviour, Jesus Christ! We are now sons of God and we have a new nature, a new identity, a divine nature. We are a new breed!

> *"But as many as received him, to them gave he power to become the sons of God, even to them that believe on his name." (John 1:12 KJV)*

Because of God's grace, we have access to His lovingkindness, getting what we don't deserve, and basking in our Father God's extravagant demonstration of love. You and I are privileged to benefit from His kindness. We are able to stand and be in His good graces! Wow, that's true love!

STANDING VS. STATE

Jesus Christ has opened the barrier between God and mankind. He is the Way.

My mother was a single parent of three when I was conceived. Her thoughts at that time were to put me up for adoption after I was born. She was overwhelmed by the fact that she was poor and didn't have the resources to take care of four children. My mother worked every day just to try to make ends meet. Her three children were old enough to be pretty self-sufficient, so she didn't need a babysitter for them while she worked. But after becoming pregnant with me, she knew she would not be able to work to take care of her children if she kept the baby, and she wouldn't have a consistent, reliable babysitter. So, she made the decision to put me up for adoption. But she told me as I grew older that after I was born and she held me, she could not bear to let me go into someone else's family. She felt she needed to be the one to raise me. I never would have known that my mom's intention was to put me up for adoption until later on in life when she shared it with me. She also shared with me that she didn't know what to name me because she had not planned to keep me.

I was born in a Catholic hospital, and while in the hospital, she heard a nurse's name spoken over the intercom. They were constantly calling, "Sister Grace Marie, Sister Grace Marie." She told me that at that point, she decided to name me Grace Marie. She truly gave me my identity when she named me Grace. She poured her love into me and I became a bona fide member of the family with all the rights and privileges. Even though we didn't have a lot, it didn't matter, because what was important to me was that I was loved and accepted with no regrets. Nothing and no one could separate me from the love of my mother, nor from the fact that I was a member of her family. Once I was accepted into the family, there was nothing I could've done that would keep me from being a part. I'm a lifetime member!

I'm sure you're wondering, what does this story have to do with my standing and my state in the family of God? God, in His infinite love and mercy, could not bear for us to be in another family that was not His. Part of His original intent when He created male and female was for them to be a part of His family, but because of sin, they were separated from Him. He could not bear for the world to be under the tutelage of this world system; He wanted us for His own, to know Him and to be a part of His family with all rights and privileges! That's why He had to redeem us through His Son, Jesus Christ.

I'm not just a sinner saved by His grace. So, who am I in Christ Jesus? What are the perks of accepting Jesus as my Lord and Saviour? According to Romans 10:9,

> *"...if you confess with your mouth the Lord Jesus and believe in your heart that God has raised Him from the dead, you will be saved." (NKJV)*

There are two areas we want to explore as it pertains to who we are in Christ Jesus, our rights as Sons and Daughters of God, and our responsibilities as part of the Family of God and Kingdom People. They are our **standing** and our **state**. It is important to understand the purpose of each one as we begin our spiritual growth process, because they are not the same.

WHERE DO YOU STAND?

Let's first explore our standing in Christ Jesus. Who are we in Christ? Our standing relates to the believer's spiritual position as it pertains to our relationship with God. Position refers to a place where someone or something is located or has been put. Therefore, our standing or position refers to our rights as sons of God. Where has God positioned us as it relates to Him? Before we knew God, we were foreigners, alienated, estranged from God because of sin. We were His enemies!

WHO ARE YOU IN CHRIST JESUS, AND
WHAT IS YOUR RESPONSIBILITY AS A BELIEVER?

"Once you were alienated from God and were enemies in your minds because of your evil behavior."
(Colossians 1:21 NIV)

But, when we accepted Jesus as our Lord and Saviour and received the Holy Spirit of promise, we were put in the position of becoming a part of the family of God. We were filled, healed, and sealed! God became our Father and thereby removed every interference that the enemy used to keep us from Him and from our relationship with Him. Our Father brought back His original intent for us. He, through the obedience of His Son, Jesus, made a way of escape for us from the practice of sin.

"Even though you were once distant from him, living in the shadows of your evil thoughts and actions, he reconnected you back to himself. He released his supernatural peace to you through the sacrifice of his own body as the sin-payment on your behalf so that you would dwell in his presence. And now there is nothing between you and Father God, for he sees you as holy, flawless, and restored." (Colossians 1:21-22 TPT)

"But those who embraced him and took hold of his name were given authority to become the children of God! He was not born by the joining of human parents or from natural means, or by a man's desire, but he was born of God." (John 1:12-13 TPT)

"For it was only through this wonderful grace that we believed in him. Nothing we did could ever earn this

> *salvation, for it was the gracious gift from God that brought us to Christ!" (Ephesians 2:8 TPT)*

As children of God, because we were purchased by the blood of the Lamb, we have rights and privileges as royalty! How about adjusting your crown!

> *"But you are a chosen generation, a **royal** priesthood, a holy nation, His own special people, that you may proclaim the praises of Him who called you out of darkness into His marvelous light." (1 Peter 2:9 NKJV)*

> *"But you are God's chosen treasure—priests who are kings, a spiritual 'nation' set apart as God's devoted ones. He called you out of darkness to experience his marvelous light, and now he claims you as his very own. He did this so that you would broadcast his glorious wonders throughout the world." (1 Peter 2:9 TPT)*

At NCCJ.org, "Privilege is unearned access to resources (social power) that are only readily available to some people because of their social group membership; an advantage, or immunity granted to or enjoyed by one societal group above and beyond the common advantage of all other groups. Privilege is often invisible to those who have it." Because of the obedience and sacrifice of our Saviour Jesus Christ, we are justified, sanctified, deemed righteous, as well as holy. As part of the family of God, our position or standing never changes. It remains constant, it remains intact. What Jesus did for us to reconcile us back to God never changes. He did what He did, and because of that, I'm positioned in God!

Our position or standing is dependent upon what Christ did for us on Calvary, not on what we've done. We can't take credit for what He did. Let's give credit where credit is due, because His blood sacrifice to cleanse us from all sin and unrighteousness was part of His finished work. We have God's righteousness at Christ's expense. You and I are sealed with the Holy Spirit of Promise. Just like my position in my natural family, it's fixed and unchanging. In the words of Stevie Wonder, I'm signed, sealed, delivered. Lord, I'm yours! It was His grace that did it.

How about that!

> *"God saved you by his grace when you believed. And you can't take credit for this; it is a gift from God. "Salvation is not a reward for the good things we have done, so none of us can boast about it." (Ephesians 2:8-9 NLT)*

> *"In Him you also trusted, after you heard the word of truth, the gospel of your salvation; in whom also, having believed, you were sealed with the Holy Spirit of promise." (Ephesians 1:13 NKJV)*

> *"And grieve not the holy Spirit of God, whereby ye are sealed unto the day of redemption."*
> *(Ephesians 4:30 KJV)*

A member of my family was adopted by his parents when he was a baby. The love and care that his parents bestowed upon him was second to none. He received their name with all the rights and privileges of being their son. It made no difference that he was not their biological son: to them and to all of us, he was a part of us, an intricate and very important part of our family, and we love him very much. Even in the court of law, he is considered a blood son. He is considered an heir.

Because of Jesus, we are heirs of God, joint heirs with Jesus Christ. How can that be? Jesus was truly God's biological son. He is the natural heir. We didn't do anything to become joint heirs with Jesus Christ. Of course we didn't! We are not God's biological children. But look at what God did for us!

> *"God decided in advance to adopt us into his own family by bringing us to himself through Jesus Christ. This is what he wanted to do, and it gave him great pleasure." (Ephesians 1:5 NLT)*

> *"But when the right time came, God sent his Son, born of a woman, subject to the law. God sent him to buy freedom for us who were slaves to the law, so that he could adopt us as his very own children. And because we are his children, God has sent the Spirit of his Son into our hearts, prompting us to call out, 'Abba, Father.' Now you are no longer a slave but God's own child. And since you are his child, God has made you his heir." (Galatians 4:4-9 NLT)*

We are now part of the family of God, and when you're part of a royal family that has wealth, you receive everything that family has to offer. You don't behave like you don't deserve to be a part of that family; no, you walk in confidence, with the authority that you are an heir to the kingdom. We came from being a pauper to now becoming a prince! We came from being rejected to becoming accepted and loved! We came from being an orphan to now being a son from a royal family. We're now royalty, saints, so now we have to behave like royalty.

> *"For all who are led by the Spirit of God are children of God. So you have not received a spirit that makes you fearful slaves. Instead, you received God's Spirit when he adopted you as his own children. Now we call him, 'Abba, Father.' For his Spirit joins with our spirit to affirm that we are God's children. And since we are his children, we are his heirs. In fact, together with Christ we are heirs of God's glory. But if we are to share his glory, we must also share his suffering." (Romans 8:14-17 NLT)*

We have an inheritance stored and waiting for us in heaven that is not defiled, nor is it decaying. It will not change. We are beneficiaries of His goodness and love through God's Son, Jesus Christ. The worth? Priceless!

> *"And we have a priceless inheritance—an inheritance that is kept in heaven for you, pure and undefiled, beyond the reach of change and decay." (1 Peter 1:4 NLT)*

We are justified by faith in Jesus Christ, which means we are forgiven of our sins, we are actually made righteous, and we have peace with God. We are no longer His enemies but now friends of God! I am a friend of God, and I am an eternal member of the Body of Christ!

> *"So now we can rejoice in our wonderful new relationship with God because our Lord Jesus Christ has made us friends of God." (Romans 5:11 NLT)*

Justification is a legal term meaning "acquittal." In our acquittal, we are declared to be right in the sight of God, even though we still have on the filthy rags of sin. Our Father does not see us that way. His Son, Jesus, paid the price for us to stand before Him acquitted! He then exchanged our filthy garments for royal garments! We have been acquitted, or freed from the penalty of death.

> *"Being justified freely by his grace through the redemption that is in Christ Jesus." (Romans 3:24 KJV)*

> *"Yet through his powerful declaration of acquittal, God freely gives away his righteousness. His gift of love and favor now cascades over us, all because Jesus, the Anointed One, has liberated us from the guilt, punishment, and power of sin!" (Romans 3:24 TPT)*

We are also sanctified. Simply put, sanctification is being "set apart." Before I came to Christ, I was an enemy of God. But when I came to Christ, He set me apart from the world and the world system which is corrupt to its core. I then began to understand the gravity of my prior situation. I'm no longer a slave to sin but set apart to be useful for the Master, to do good works.

> *"By God's will we have been purified and made holy once and for all through the sacrifice of the body of Jesus, the Messiah!" (Hebrews 10:10 TPT)*

> *"...Your life and ministry must not be disgraced, for you are to be a pure container of Christ and dedicated to the honorable purposes of your Master, prepared for every good work that he gives you to do." (2 Timothy 2:21 TPT)*

My standing in God never changes, but my state can!

MUSING: THOUGHTS TO PROVOKE

"As long as a believer is worrying about whether or not they are truly saved, they will never grow up in spiritual maturity. It basically guarantees that a Christian will remain stuck in spiritual infancy. And worse, it paints a picture of God that is not only untrue but also unbiblical. It cheapens the gift of salvation – the gift of grace – and makes God look like a finicky human." – Will Davis Jr.

QUESTIONS TO PONDER:

How have my views changed concerning my relationship with Jesus and my standing in Him?

WHAT STATE ARE YOU IN?
"LOCATION, LOCATION, LOCATION!"

My standing refers to who I am in Christ Jesus, but my state refers to who I am in my heart, my mind, my will, my emotions as it pertains to God. Dictionary.com defines state as "the particular condition that someone or something is in at a specific time." Therefore, my state refers to my condition. Merriam-Webster's dictionary defines condition as a verb meaning "to modify so that an act or response previously associated with one stimulus becomes associated with another." In other words, my state or condition can change depending upon what I allow to stimulate me. So, which way do I go? Do I allow my flesh to reign and go my own way, or do I allow God to reign and go His way?

After I come to Christ, my position is set. It never changes, but my condition, my state of being, can definitely change. In the same way, my physical body can definitely change depending upon what I do to it and for it. God made our bodies to heal themselves. But we can change all that by what we eat, if we exercise, and if we ingest alcohol or drugs.

Personally, I've had problems with my weight. It fluctuates. One of the hats that I wear is that of an educator, and I've noticed that during the school year, I am more mobile and more apt to either lose weight or at least stay at a decent weight, because I'm watching what I eat, taking my vitamins, and staying on the go. But oh, when summer comes and school is out, I begin to eat comfort foods more – you know, the foods like chips and sweets. Besides not giving myself what my body needs nutritionally, I'm not on the go as much either. As a result, my weight goes back up until I go back to work. So, the state that I am in changes constantly depending on what I do.

It is my responsibility to change myself. It is no one else's responsibility to deal with my weight fluctuation but mine and mine alone. Now, on the other hand, I can submit myself to someone like a nutritionist or a physical trainer to coach me so that I can keep my weight from fluctuating. But again, it is not their responsibility but mine to listen to them and do what they recommend. They can't make me eat correctly or exercise consistently. I have to take the initiative to seek help and do what that help recommends. It is my choice, and I have the freedom of will to make it. I always say that one of the greatest gifts that God gave mankind is the freedom to choose.

So, our state relates not to who we are in Christ Jesus – that's our standing – but to who we are in ourselves and with ourselves. It is what we practice. It is our walk before ourselves and others. I may say that I am a child of God purchased by the blood of the Lamb and I have my sonship rights, but does this child of God's behavior with family, friends, co-workers, and the world match my standing in Christ? The state we're in also pertains to our work or service to the Lord after our salvation. The Apostle Paul said it best:

> *"My beloved ones, just like you've always listened to everything I've taught you in the past, I'm asking you now to keep following my instructions as though I were right there with you. Now you must continue to make this new life fully manifested as you live in the holy awe of God—which brings you trembling into his presence. God will continually revitalize you, implanting within you the passion to do what pleases him." (Philippians 2:12-13 TPT)*

This is where my spiritual growth happens. It happens in the state that I'm in, and my state can fluctuate. This is the place where my renewed mind walk occurs. If I want to be more and more like Jesus, if I'm to have  authentic spiritual growth and maturity, this is the place where I have to take the responsibility to use all that God has available for me in His Word, those that He puts in my life to aid in my spiritual maturation, His grace that enables me to do it, and His Holy Spirit that directs me in it!

"...Since, then, we do not have the excuse of ignorance, everything—and I do mean everything—connected with that old way of life has to go. It's rotten through and through. Get rid of it! And then take on an entirely new way of life—a God-fashioned life, a life renewed from the inside and working itself into your conduct as God accurately reproduces his character in you." (Ephesians 4:20-24 MSG)

MUSING: THOUGHTS TO PROVOKE

"The more you reaffirm who you are in Christ, the more your behavior will begin to reflect your true identity." Neil T. Anderson.

QUESTIONS TO PONDER:

What state are you in, and are you satisfied? If you're satisfied with the state you're in, how are you going to make it even better? If you're not satisfied, what areas of your life need to be in a better state, and what steps are you going to make to get there?

CHAPTER 3:
SPIRITUAL MATURITY

"Make that change, be that change!"
– Grace Blue

John MacArthur, in his blog, speaks about the gift of salvation in Philippians 2:12, which was given by God alone, but he also talks about the responsibility of the believer. He relates the story of Strabo, an ancient Roman scholar who lived about sixty years before Christ, and his account regarding some Roman-owned mines in Spain. MacArthur writes that Strabo "uses the very same verb that Paul does in Philippians 2:12, the Greek word *katergazomai,* when referring to the Romans as *working out* the mines. Strabo's point was that the Romans were extracting from within the mines all their richness and value."

MacArthur goes on to say: "That's a fitting expression of what *katergazomai* (work out) means in Philippians 2:12. *I am to mine out of my life what God has richly deposited there in salvation. I am to produce such precious nuggets of godly character from what He planted when He saved me."*

Mining out of my life the rich nuggets of godly character by growing spiritually is my responsibility, not God's! I have to assess the state that I'm in, because my standing in God is secure.

When I came to Christ, I was born again. I didn't come to Christ as a fully matured Christian; I came into the Family of God as a newborn babe. Once I came to Christ, I had to begin the process of replacing the old mindset of Adam's nature with the divine nature and renewed mindset of Christ Jesus. Remember what Jesus told Nicodemus when he came to Jesus by night asking questions. Jesus answered him by paralleling the processes of natural and the spiritual birth.

> *"Jesus answered, 'Nicodemus, listen to this eternal truth: Before a person can perceive God's kingdom realm, they must first experience a rebirth.' Nicodemus said, 'Rebirth? How can a gray-headed man be reborn? It's impossible for a man to go back into the womb a second time and be reborn!' Jesus answered, 'I speak an eternal truth: Unless you are born of water and Spirit-wind, you will never enter God's kingdom realm. For the natural realm can only give birth to things that are natural, but the spiritual realm gives birth to supernatural life! You shouldn't be amazed by my statement, "You must be born from above!"'" (John 3:3-7 TPT)*

In a natural birth, a baby does not come out of its mother's womb a fully grown adult. It comes out as a baby that needs to be nurtured and nourished, and over time, it physically develops into a mature adult. From the time we're conceived, we move from dependence to independence, and then to interdependence.

Spiritual birth is the same way. When we come to Christ, we come as babes in Christ. We are spiritually immature. As babies, we need to be nurtured and nourished, and over time, we will develop into spiritually mature adults. From the time we're born again, we are also to move from dependence to independence, and then to interdependence. I'll expound more on how this works later.

There are different types of growth that we experience in our life, including physical, mental, career, social, and spiritual growth. Each one, if you are vigilant, will lead you to maturity and productivity.

Spiritual growth, as in natural growth, involves development and improvement towards a goal of maturity. With growth and development, changes must take place. As a part of spiritually maturing, we can no longer cater to the Kingdom of Self, but we must wholeheartedly give ourselves to the expansion of the Kingdom of God.

Our goal should be to come to a level of maturity that is spoken of in the Word of God. That word *maturity* spoken of in scripture is the Greek word "teleios." According to Strong's Concordance, "teleios" can be described as "genuine, complete, finish, fulfil, accomplished, perfect, having reached its end, fully grown, fully developed."

When we come to this level of spiritual maturity, it demonstrates that we are genuinely fully grown and fully developed in Christ. This is the will of God for the life of the Believer. We must grow up and grow deep if we are truly going to do as Jesus commanded us to do, go and make disciples!

> *"Stop imitating the ideals and opinions of the culture around you, but be inwardly transformed by the Holy Spirit through a total reformation of how you think. This will empower you to discern God's will as you live a beautiful life, satisfying and perfect [teleios] in his eyes." (Romans 12:2 TPT)*

> *"Beloved ones, don't remain as immature children in your reasoning. As it relates to evil, be like newborns, but in your thinking be mature adults [teleios]." (1 Corinthians 14:20 TPT)*

The Christian author Jay E. Adams describes growth as "changing into the fulness of the stature of Christ." If we were to define authentic spiritual growth, it is a true and actual process of removing wrong ideas, concepts, mindsets, thoughts, beliefs, and ideas that are contrary to the Word, the Will, and the Ways of God, as well as developing our awareness of who we are in Christ Jesus and becoming more and more like Him because we will see and know Him as He is. Authentic spiritual growth has to be meaningful and deliberate. When we find that our ideas, concepts, mindsets, thoughts, beliefs, and ideas don't match up with God's Word, Will, and Way, we must do the inward work of aligning our ways to His ways! In other words, as Michael Jackson sang, look at the man in the mirror and make that change!

SPIRITUAL MATURITY

"These grace ministries will function until we all attain oneness in the faith, until we all experience the fullness of what it means to know the Son of God, and finally we become one perfect [teleios] man with the full dimensions of spiritual maturity [teleios] and fully developed in the abundance of Christ." (Ephesians 4:13 TPT)

MUSING: THOUGHTS TO PROVOKE

"Spiritual maturity is not reached by the passing of the years, but by obedience to the will of God. Some people mature into an understanding of God's will more quickly than others because they obey more readily; they more readily sacrifice the life of nature to the will of God."
– Oswald Chambers

QUESTIONS TO PONDER:

How are you mining out the rich gold nuggets of your life in Christ?

YOU ARE RESPONSIBLE!

Our spiritual growth and maturity is determined by our daily choices. This is the place in our spiritual walk where we receive rewards or consequences with the choices we make. You and I are each responsible for our own spiritual growth and maturity. If we are content with being Butts in the Seats, Pigs in the Pen, or Baby Hueys, then we will never experience the more abundant life that Jesus promised in John 10:10. We will instead allow the enemy to steal, kill, and destroy God's purpose, plan, and assignment for our lives. As a result, we will continue to be frustrated Christians, never fully experiencing a relationship with the Father and His promises for us, nor will we fully walk in our purpose.

> *"And now, beloved brothers and sisters, since you have been mentored by us with respect to living for God and pleasing him, I appeal to you in the name of the Lord Jesus with this request: keep faithfully growing through our teachings even more and more."* (1 Thessalonians 4:1-2 TPT)

God has fully given us everything we need to successfully walk this Christian walk in sincerity and godliness. It's really easy to point fingers at other people when we see their flaws and failures, but we can be in denial or blame others concerning our own flaws and failures. I can't blame my husband, my children, my pastor, the boss on my job, my friends, my co-workers, race, government, God, Jesus Christ, or even the devil. We may even try to blame the church we attend. People will use the church to justify doing "the hop" – you know, the church hop, going from one church to another but never fully committing to one. But keep in mind, the church can create an environment conducive for spiritual growth by teaching members the importance of attending Bible Study and Sunday School, and encouraging them to have a time of worship and communion with God. Teach them how to release the power of God and walk in newness of mind. The church you attend may even have a means of accountability through discipleship. But it's still our choice to take the responsibility to participate in our own authentic spiritual growth and development. Our all-powerful Father God has given us everything that pertains to life and godliness. The closer we get to Him, the more we will know Him and experience His glory and excellence.

"Everything we could ever need for life and complete devotion to God has already been deposited in us by his divine power. For all this was lavished upon us through the rich experience of knowing him who has called us by name and invited us to come to him through a glorious manifestation of his goodness." (2 Peter 1:3 TPT)

A poem attributed to the 16th century philosopher Francis Bacon sums up the fact that we have the responsibility to act, not just talk:

> *"It's not what we eat but what we digest that makes us strong; not what we gain but what we save that makes us rich; not what we read but what we remember that makes us learned; and not what we profess but what we practice that gives us integrity."*

It boils down to our integrity. Integrity is gained by what we do, not by what we say.

The American author Jim George says, "Spiritual maturity is a lifelong pursuit. We grow in spiritual maturity moment by moment, day by day, year by year." In other words, growing is not something that is done overnight, but step by step, inch by inch, it's a cinch to grow in and with His grace!

MUSING: THOUGHTS TO PROVOKE

"It is no one else's responsibility to avoid my triggers. It is not the government's responsibility to redesign the nation so I don't get triggered. It is not a business's job to make sure they don't say anything that triggers me. It's not my spouse's responsibility to walk on eggshells so I don't blow up. It's not my kid's responsibility to behave in such a way I don't go off on them. It's my responsibility to make sure I don't have bullets loaded in my heart so no matter what happens around me I respond in a healthy way." – Seth Dahl

QUESTIONS TO PONDER:

What triggers do I have that I need to take responsibility for and remove? What strategies will I develop for removing them?

MOVEMENT VS. STAGNATION

As Pastors, along with the other Five-Fold ministries spoken of in Ephesians 4, our job is to ensure that we are teaching people to know God and His Word, to help lead them to know what God wants them to do, and to train them on how to do what God wants them to do. In my role as co-pastor of a wonderful church with wonderful people, I experienced the good, the

bad, and the ugly of pastoring. The good was when my husband and I saw believers who didn't point fingers at why they were in the spiritual condition or state they were in, but recognized they could do something to change their state – they didn't have to stay the same. They began the spiritual growth process. They assessed themselves and realized they wanted more. They believed the Word of God and didn't make excuses for themselves. We observed such spiritual growth and maturity with them. Now, don't get me wrong, it wasn't that they didn't make mistakes or didn't fail, but what we admired in them was their perseverance and their determination to become more and more like Christ. They came for help when they needed it. They took correction even when they didn't like or appreciate it. They developed a prayer life and intimacy with God. They used the resources that God had available.

But then there was the bad of pastoring. This happens when a pastor sees a member they know can go far in God, but their pride keeps them from admitting that a renewed mind is the key to their success. They blame others or circumstances as justification for staying in a dark place. A pastor can see them going through the same cycles of despair, disappointment, sin, and fear. As a pastor, you are doing all that you know to help them break the cycle, but it takes a made-up mind and a person who decides they're not going to blame anyone nor anything, not even themselves, but will take the initiative to make the necessary changes.

The ugly of pastoring comes when those you pastor blame you for their missteps and leave the church, constantly lambasting the pastor and the church for a myriad of reasons. A couple of the phrases they may use are "I'm not being fed," or "They're holding me back from ministry," or "They're picking on me." Then you have those who don't think they have been fed enough to walk in their destiny and fulfill the purpose of God for their lives. So, you're constantly feeding them, and they're constantly eating and eating and eating, getting fat in the Word and staying a turkey or a chicken, but never trying to fly like an eagle!

You can have people in the same church hearing the same Word of God but personally experiencing it differently. When you see people who believe it's more important to be firmly and deeply rooted in God than in anything else, that's when you see authentic spiritual growth and maturity.

> *"Wickedness never brings stability, but the godly have deep roots." (Proverbs 12:3 NLT)*

There is an old story about an alcoholic father who had two sons. They grew into young men, and one son became an alcoholic. "What choice do I have?" he said. "My father is an alcoholic."

The other son never touched a drop of alcohol. "How could I?" he said. "Look what it did to my father." Two sons, same dad, but different perspectives and different outcomes.

I remember the animated movie by Disney called *Finding Nemo*. For those of you who are not familiar, it's about a young clownfish named Nemo who lived in the deep blue sea and got lost and separated from his dad, Marlin. Marlin spends the whole movie on a quest to find his son. He meets up with a fish named Dory, who has short-term memory loss but could always seem to remember to remind Marlin, when he got discouraged during his quest to find his son, to keep swimming. Dory encourages Marlin not to give up but to continue on his journey to find his son.

In the same way, we have to beware of stagnation when it pertains to our spiritual growth. Stagnation refers to little or no movement or flow. For example, stagnant water is a breeding ground for mosquitoes that carry disease, bacterial growth, and algae, which chokes off the growth of other life forms, produces mold, and causes the rotting of plants and organisms that lived in the water. What happens when a person has little or no movement? My husband, James, humorously calls it constipation. You know what happens to your insides when you're constipated! Others often call those with little or no movement couch potatoes. They sit and watch TV, and the only time they get up is to get some food or go to the bathroom. When there is no movement, circulation in the body slows down, oxygen decreases, toxins build up, and sickness happens! So, spiritual stagnation is when a Christian has no movement in God. They have been the same since they first came to the Lord. There is no change, no movement, no progress. The unfortunate thing about it is that they may be content to remain the same. But others may have no movement not because they want to stay the same, but because they don't know how to grow in His grace.

> *"Those who do not move, do not notice their chains."*
> – Rosa Luxemburg

In order to overcome stagnation, we must do as Dory suggested: keep swimming! Let's keep moving, keep growing through adversity, through uncertainties, through missteps, because when we do, we shall experience the power of God, the intimacy with God, the knowledge of God, the grace of God in such a way that it spills over into the lives of those we come in contact with.

> **MUSING: THOUGHTS TO PROVOKE**
>
> "Be not afraid of growing slowly, be afraid only of standing still." – Chinese Proverb
>
> **QUESTIONS TO PONDER:**
>
> What am I doing, or what do I need to do, so that I don't become or remain stagnant? What areas of my life do I feel are moving and growing?

IF YOU WANNA GROW, RENEW YOUR MIND!

"And be renewed in the spirit of your mind."
(Ephesians 4:23 KJV)

"So keep your thoughts continually fixed on all that is authentic and real, honorable and admirable, beautiful and respectful, pure and holy, merciful and kind. And fasten your thoughts on every glorious work of God, praising him always." (Philippians 4:8 TPT)

In my experience as a Christian and as a Pastor/Apostle, I have found that many Christians think that what's keeping them from all that God has for them is rooted in outside influences.

Many believers use that excuse for a reason not to grow, not to experience authentic change and transformation. But that's only a small part of the reason.

Our mind is the organ of thought. God created our minds to think, reason, understand, imagine, and remember. The mind's storage capacity is mind-boggling. The mind is very influential; in fact, it influences our every action. So, our mind is the real battlefield! Our mind is where the enemy of our soul loves to take up residence and reign.

BOOM! BANG BANG! BAM! KABOOM! CLASH!

These words can all be considered sounds of war or conflict. We are definitely waging war, Saints. This war that we're waging is not with flesh and blood, but it's a spiritual battle, spiritual warfare. In fact, the battle that is being waged starts in our minds.

Why is that so significant? Isaiah 26:3 says,

> *"You will keep him in perfect peace, Whose mind is stayed on You, Because he trusts in You." (NKJV)*

The word *mind* in this scripture is translated from the Hebrew word "yester," which means framework or framing. The mind is like a framed house that is meant to shelter, a place to abide. When God created man and woman, He intended for the mind to be a place of habitation, a place to communicate with Him and to commune with Him, a place to create as well as to imagine. The mind was to be a place where we would house the thoughts and plans that God has for us and those that come in our path. The devil knew that. That's why he fights so hard to keep our minds away from God and His Word: God fashioned our minds to be in concert with His mind.

Keep in Isaiah 26:3 is the Hebrew word "natsar," which means to maintain, to protect, to form a blockade. When our mind is stayed on God, He will protect, guard, and maintain us, and block the enemy from gaining a toehold, a foothold, or a stronghold against us. God forms a blockade between our minds and our enemy the devil. God is certainly a keeper. That's something special to shout about!

Perfect peace in that same scripture is so interesting, because both of those words, *perfect* and *peace*, are from the Hebrew word "Shalom." He will keep us in double Shalom, which would read "Shalom, Shalom": double peace. In the One New Man Bible, it says that "Shalom cannot be translated into English with a single word. The word Shalom comes from the word 'Shalem' which means complete. When there is Shalom there is tranquility, justice, peace, sufficiency, divine health, absence of disorder, injustice, conflict, and all other negative forces." A rabbi once wrote that Shalom means "No good thing is withheld." So, when we keep the house of our minds propped up on Him, He keeps us in double peace! We must keep Him as the foundation. That's why the combat that the devil wages in our minds is so fierce, because he knows that in the shelter of my mind, I can have double shalom if I keep my mind on Him.

According to Strong's Concordance, the word *stayed* in the Hebrew, "samak," means "to bear up, prop up, establish, (up-)hold, lay, lean, lie hard, put, rest self, set self, stand fast, stay (self), sustain."

When I keep my mind stayed on Him, it means I lean hard on him, I stand fast on Him and His Word; I prop myself up on Him and not on myself or anyone else. I depend on Him, not on myself nor others, and He in turn is the support and the brace that I need to ensure my double peace is intact.

The battle in and for our minds is the greatest opposition to our living the more abundant life and bringing that life and presence of the Lord to others. Remember, it's not just about us; it's also about touching the lives of others and becoming that powerfully anointed epistle that is read by others (2 Corinthians 3:2-3). That is done by the measure of our maturity that we allow to transform our lives.

> *"For we wrestle not against flesh and blood, but against principalities, against powers, against the rulers of the darkness of this world, against spiritual wickedness in high places." (Ephesians 6:12 KJV)*

> *"Your hand-to-hand combat is not with human beings, but with the highest principalities and authorities operating in rebellion under the heavenly realms. For they are a powerful class of demon-gods and evil spirits that hold this dark world in bondage." (Ephesians 6:12 TPT)*

The devil wants our minds, our will, and our emotions. He wants to entangle and control them enough to incapacitate us, in order to render us powerless, hopeless, and useless, especially in the areas God has called us to. The devil knows that God has plans for us, plans to prosper us and bring us to success. The war that we wage in our minds against our enemy is the invisible war. It cannot be seen with the naked eye, but Saints of God, the spiritual combat is real!

There was a time early in my life as Co-Pastor when I was tricked by evil spiritual forces through my thoughts, to the point of believing that the financial hardship that my family was consistently facing at the time was the will of God. Now, mind you, I never said or expressed those thoughts verbally. I knew, since I had become a Christian and learned the Word of God, that God meant for us to prosper and that Jesus came that we might have a more abundant life. But because I decided to believe the lies of the enemy, I disannulled the Word of God in my own heart and mind. Of course, I never believed those lies of the enemy for others. I believed the Word of God for them concerning prosperity, but I didn't believe it for myself. The funny thing about it is, if you had asked me, I would have told you what the Word of God said, and I really thought I believed it. There was controversy! The controversy was that what was going on in my mind was in direct contrast and contradiction to what the Word of God said. I allowed a foreign entity to invade my thoughts and mind. Just as Eve, in the Garden of God, was lied to and believed the lies of the devil, I was lied to and believed his lies. Unknowingly, in my mind I allowed the devil to take a toehold, then a foothold, and if that wasn't enough, he took a stronghold of an area of my mind that I had no idea he had. The devil is greedy. He wants it all!

> *"But I am afraid that just as Eve was deceived by the serpent's cunning, your minds may somehow be led astray from your sincere and pure devotion to Christ." (2 Corinthians 11:3 NIV)*

There's a saying that I found based upon Mark 4:23:

"It's not enough to hear My words, you have to allow them to change the way you live." – God

My mind had come into agreement with the lies of the enemy. It had gotten to the point that my own actions mirrored what was going on in my mind. The enemy of my soul had built a stronghold concerning my finances. Until!

I was one of the camp directors at a summer camp that our churches held each summer. This particular time, there were some ladies who came to one of the nightly services. I hadn't seen these ladies in many years, and we were so happy to reunite. After service was over, they left and went back home, which was quite a distance. The next day, they came back to the camp during the day and said to me that God had told them to come back and minister to me. I, of course, was puzzled, thinking, "What's wrong with me?" I actually thought I was fine. But God in His infinite love and mercy for me said otherwise. They asked me if they could minister to me, and I answered yes. That was the best decision that I ever could have made. Thank God I was wise enough to answer in the affirmative. Well, as they began to minister to me, they started pulling down strongholds that had held my mind in captivity. I began to let go and allow God to tear apart those ideas and mindsets that held me captive, especially in the area of prosperity. After they pulled down those strongholds of lies, they began to speak prophetic words into my life. Words that spoke to God's original intent for me and my life. How the enemy of my soul tried to steal my identity through my thoughts and ideas about myself and my situation. I began to sense and feel the release of my mind, my heart, and my emotions. The best way to describe what happened was that I felt like I came back to myself. I finally felt freedom that I didn't know I needed! This was a time when I was in bondage but didn't realize it.

You may say, "You mean a Pastor can need deliverance?" You bet your life we can! What better group for the devil to get a stronghold on than those leaders who influence the lives of others? If he can entangle leaders, his net is wider to entangle those who are influenced by the leader. As stated before, our archenemy the devil wants to build a stronghold in our minds because he knows that "how goes the mind, goes the body." Remember, our fight is not with flesh and blood but with evil hidden spiritual figures that are out to steal, kill, and destroy our minds, our hearts, our purpose, our relationships, and the assignment that God put us on this planet to complete for His Glory!

> *"For although we live in the natural realm, we don't wage a military campaign employing human weapons, using manipulation to achieve our aims. Instead, our spiritual weapons are energized with divine power to effectively dismantle the defenses behind which people hide. We can demolish every deceptive fantasy that opposes God and break through every arrogant attitude that is raised up in defiance of the true knowledge of God. We capture, like prisoners of war, every thought and insist that it bow in obedience to the Anointed One." (2 Corinthians 10:3-5 TPT)*

That's why the Apostle Paul urges us to put on the Armor of God in Ephesians 6:11-18. If we want to overcome the deceptions of the devil, we have to make sure we have on truth, righteousness, the gospel of peace, faith, and salvation, and above all, carry inside of us the Word of God fortified with prayer.

Let's delve into the meaning of strongholds. Strong's Concordance states that the word *stronghold* in the Bible is from the Greek word "ochurama," which means a fortress, a castle, or a citadel. In the New Testament, it's described as a prison. The Apostle Paul refers to strongholds as lies that the devil has ingrained so deeply in the mind, emotions, and belief system that he now exerts power over certain areas of a person's life. The devil attempts to build strong lies in your mind so that he can rule from a high, overbearing position in your thoughts and emotions. When there is a stronghold in your thoughts and emotions, you will begin to manifest those thoughts and emotions in the flesh. Demonic spirits are out to sabotage the will of God for your life, and the power of God in your life, by any means necessary. He's out to destroy your reputation in order to render you lifeless and hopeless. The devil's aim is to imprison you and me. He wants to be a jailer, holding the keys to the prison doors that have our mind confined. Demonic forces would have us sitting behind mental and emotional bars. The enemy is within! So, let's take him out!!

> *"Be alert and of sober mind. Your enemy the devil prowls around like a roaring lion looking for someone to devour."*
> *(1 Peter 5:8 NIV)*

The late author Adrian Rogers proposed that "Satan's desire is to conquer and control your thought life, and then make it a citadel from which he can war against God. But, when God saved you, He gave you the mind of Christ."

Jesus has already said that the devil is a liar and the truth is not in him. The devil's cunningness is that he plants thoughts in our minds anticipating that we will take them as our own, engage with them, embrace them, and make them our own. The thought then becomes activated in our lives. Our minds are Satan's target, and when he gets a stronghold, he uses us to make God's Word of no effect. It becomes null and void in our lives. His aim is to keep us in a place of stagnation so we are not able to grow authentically in Christ.

It's been said that the enemy is not after your money or your stuff. He wants your mind, your attitude, your heart, your faith, your peace. If taking your money or your stuff affects your mind and emotions in a negative way, the enemy of your soul will use them to control your mind and emotions. Understand that you're not being attacked over the tangible things in your life. The enemy is fighting you over the things you can't see but know are in your mind and your heart. That's why it's important to renew our minds daily, because the crafty demonic spirits are constantly coming for your mind and mine. We must build a spiritual barricade in our minds against the enemy so he cannot infiltrate them to set up a stronghold there.

> *"And be not conformed to this world: but be ye transformed by the renewing of your mind, that ye may prove what is that good, and acceptable, and perfect, will of God."* (Romans 12:2 KJV)

I love the different translations of Romans 12:2:

> *"And do not imitate this world, but be transformed by the renovation of your minds, and you shall distinguish what is the good, acceptable and perfect will of God." (Aramaic Bible in Plain English)*

> *"Don't become like the people of this world. Instead, change the way you think. Then you will always be able to determine what God really wants—what is good, pleasing, and perfect." (God's Word Translation)*

> *"Stop imitating the ideals and opinions of the culture around you, but be inwardly transformed by the Holy Spirit through a total reformation of how you think. This will empower you to discern God's will as you live a beautiful life, satisfying and perfect in his eyes." (TPT)*

According to these translations of this verse, we have to renovate and reform our minds by changing the way we think. Paul tells us not to fashion our way of thinking according to that of the world. The word *transformed* is translated from the Greek "metamorphose," which means to change, transfigure, reshape, mature. It's like a caterpillar changing into a beautiful butterfly.

The good news is that we have power to overcome our enemy the devil! These strongholds can be eliminated and destroyed, not by fleshly means, but by the power of the spiritual weapons supplied by the Holy Spirit.

> *"I pray that you will continually experience the immeasurable greatness of God's power made available to you through faith. Then your lives will be an advertisement of this immense power as it works through you! This is the mighty power that was released when God raised Christ*

> *from the dead and exalted him to the place of highest honor and supreme authority in the heavenly realm!"*
>
> *(Ephesians 1:19-20 TPT)*

The cognitive neuroscientist Dr. Caroline Leaf says, "As we think, we change the physical nature of our brain. As we consciously direct our thinking, we can wire out toxic patterns of thinking and replace them with healthy thoughts."

From my own experiences, I have learned the importance of renewing my mind daily. That means I have to self-check and fact check. I have to make sure that the devil is not infiltrating my mind with fake news about myself or other people. I have to assess myself to see if my thinking and my actions match up to the Word of God, the Will of God, and the Ways of God! Again, I have to take the responsibility. That in itself is part of the authentic spiritual growth process.

> *"If you listen to the Word and don't live out the message you hear, you become like the person who looks in the mirror of the Word to discover the reflection of his face in the beginning. You perceive how God sees you in the mirror of the Word, but then you go out and forget your divine origin. But those who set their gaze deeply into the perfecting law of liberty are fascinated by and respond to the truth they hear and are strengthened by it—they experience God's blessing in all that they do!"*
> *(James 1:23-25 TPT)*

The state that I'm in is determined by how much responsibility I take to assess myself and make the necessary steps to change myself. I must take the responsibility to know when to self-assess, and if I find that my mind and/or my heart is not in alignment with His Word, His Will, and His Way, then I need to be wise and humble myself enough to renew my mind and heart! On the other hand, as I do my self-check, I may find that my heart and mind are in alignment with the will of God. But the important thing is to self-check!

So, as I mature, my flesh – which is my mind, my will, my emotions, my body, and my heart – takes more of a backseat, and I allow the Spirit of God that's in me to sit in the driver's seat. Because the Spirit of God knows where I need to go, why I need to go there, the path I need to take, and the speed limit that I'm to travel.

MUSING: THOUGHTS TO PROVOKE

"It is as though there is a splinter working its way to the surface, only this splinter is in your soul. And just as the skin wants a foreign object gone and pushes it out, the soul wants to be healthy and will not leave you in peace until you stop drenching it with the poisons of your feelings about the past." – Stephen Mansfield

QUESTIONS TO PONDER:

What do I need to do to get and keep my thinking in alignment with the Word, Will, and Way of God?

CHAPTER 4:
DEVELOPMENTAL STAGES OF THE SONS OF GOD

How do we determine the stages of development? We live, we go through life, then we die. Is that all there is to life? Of course not!

Growing old is inevitable, but growing up with grace in His grace is a choice.

> *"When granted many years of life, growing old in age is natural, but growing old with grace is a choice. Growing older with grace is possible for all who will set their hearts and minds on the Giver of grace, the Lord Jesus Christ."*
> *– Billy Graham*

God has set a course for each of us to run in this life, and we must run this race with faith, purpose, endurance, perseverance, and obedience, with our eyes firmly fixed on Jesus. Part of this life's marathon is going through stages of spiritual growth and maturity. When we are born again, we are not automatically transformed into mature Believers in Christ. Instead, as in our physical lives, we begin our Christian journey through the spiritual stages of growth as babes in Christ. God's intention for authentic spiritual growth and maturation is for us to develop in stages.

> *"...So we must let go of every wound that has pierced us and the sin we so easily fall into. Then we will be able to run life's marathon race with passion and determination, for the path has been already marked out before us. We look away from the natural realm and we fasten our gaze onto Jesus who birthed faith within us and who leads us forward into faith's perfection. His example is this: Because his heart was focused on the joy of knowing that you would be his, he endured the agony of the cross and conquered its humiliation, and now sits exalted at the right hand of the throne of God!" (Hebrews 12:1-2 TPT)*

There are three stages of life that I mentioned earlier: dependent, independent, and interdependent.

The first stage is dependence. In this stage, a person relies on others to support them and give them wisdom and direction. They are receiving information and learning, and they have not yet come into their own as a person. During this stage of life, a person is learning about their surroundings, who they are, and what they can do.

In the independent stage of life, a person comes into their own. They take the wisdom and knowledge they learned in the dependent stage and decide what they're going to use. They are developing their values and learning to articulate them.

Then there is the interdependent stage, which it has been said many people don't reach because it takes a higher level of maturity to attain. It requires that a person be neither self-centered nor selfish. A person realizes they are connected to others, whether they be family, friends, co-workers, or members of the community. In this stage of life, one begins to freely share their wisdom with others and also receive the wisdom of others. You see me and receive what I have, and I see you and receive what you have. We are linked together. That's true interdependence and community!

According to the author Nina Simon, "A community is a group of people who share something in common. You can define a community by the shared attributes of the people in it and/or by the strength of the connections among them. You need a bunch of people who are alike in some way, who feel some sense of belonging or interpersonal connection."

The first-century church in chapter 2 of the book of Acts certainly understood and practiced interdependence and community. They shared what they had with each other and didn't hold back. Interdependence birthed community.

> *"All the believers were in fellowship as one body, and they shared with one another whatever they had. Out of generosity they even sold their assets to distribute the proceeds to those who were in need among them. Daily they met together in the temple courts and in one another's homes to celebrate communion. They shared meals together with joyful hearts and tender humility. They were*

> *continually filled with praises to God, enjoying the favor of all the people. And the Lord kept adding to their number daily those who were coming to life." (Acts 2:44-47 TPT)*

Stephen R. Covey sums up dependence, independence, and interdependence by stating in his book The *7 Habits of Highly Effective People,* "Dependent people need others to get what they want. Independent people can get what they want through their own effort. Interdependent people combine their own efforts with the efforts of others to achieve their greatest success." He also says, "Interdependence is a choice only independent people can make."

Watching my own children go through these three stages of life really helped me understand and experience the differences firsthand. I watched as they went through the stage of dependence. They relied upon their dad and me for everything. From the time they were in my womb, they thought we were the best thing since sliced bread. They depended upon us for nourishment, protection, guidance, encouragement, and support. They looked to us as their role models. My husband and I sacrificed a lot for the well-being of our offspring because we loved them, we knew we were their source, and they depended upon us to supply their every need. That was our role as parents whose children depended upon us.

Then there was a time, especially when they reached puberty and adolescence, when they were stretching their need for independence. They no longer thought of their parents as ones who knew everything, could do anything, and would provide for them in every way. In fact, many times, they thought we knew absolutely nothing and our opinions weren't that valuable. They began to stretch their wings of independence by making their own choices and stating their own opinions. Sometimes we agreed with the decisions they made, and then there were times when we thought they had just plain lost their minds.

Now that they've become mature adults, my husband and I are experiencing a time of interdependence with our adult children. This is a time when we can depend on each other – there is an exchange! If we have a need, our adult children are in a position to help us. This takes maturity. If they were selfish, then even though they have the means, their selfishness would not allow them to help us. If they have a need, my husband and I have the means to assist them. We can combine our resources and achieve success. We're loving this time of interdependence that we're experiencing with our own mature adult children. It is a true blessing!

As we delve further into authentic spiritual growth by looking at these three developmental stages, you will be able to assess where you are in your spiritual growth and maturation process and what you need to do to change the state that you're in.

I'm going to use the example of the natural stages of development to explain the spiritual stages of development and growth. In the next sections and the following two chapters, I use Greek words for "children/child/son" as headings because I believe they best describe the characteristics of those particular stages of spiritual maturation and growth. All of the Greek words that I use as headings refer to a Believer as a child or son of God. I also believe it's so important to understand where each of us is in our spiritual growth journey so that we can confidently press on toward that high calling in Jesus Christ.

I first started studying and teaching spiritual growth in one of our church conferences, then as a midweek online Bible Study. The Holy Spirit had me title it "Growing in Grace with Grace." The Holy Spirit laid it in my lap and on my heart to teach it and then to write a book about it. I know, I know, there are plenty of books and articles on spiritual growth. I thought and said the same thing, but the Lord told me that the direction He's taking me with the writing of this book is what is needed now in the Body of Christ like never before.

> *"For everything there is a season, and a time for every matter under heaven." (Ecclesiastes 3:1 ESV)*

Every day, we should be changing; we cannot reach full maturity unless we do. Even in the physical, our bodies change. Our bodies are constantly changing from conception until we grow old and die. We don't have any choice in our bodies changing; it happens automatically. God has structured our physical bodies to change, to grow, to mature. We really don't have any say-so in the matter unless, during our physical body's growth process, we cooperate with the plan of God, which is for the healthy growth of our bodies. We do that by eating the right types of food, exercising, and making sure we don't put any foreign substances in our bodies that will cause it to deteriorate faster.

My mother recently passed away. It was such a blessing to be able to take care of her in her declining years. When she left us, she was in her one hundredth year. She passed away in January of 2020 and would have been one hundred on her birthday in May of that same year. Many people would ask me about the key to my mom's longevity. I thought about it, and in all the years that I observed my mom, especially after she made Jesus Lord of her life, she didn't smoke, she didn't do drugs or drink alcohol, she kept her body moving, and she ate healthy and took her supplements. She made a point to forgive, so she didn't hold grudges. She studied the scriptures daily and was a mighty prayer warrior. When my mom left this earth, she was not on any medications, and she was in her right mind and always called on Jesus. She was certainly one who took care of her body, her soul, and her spirit. Thanks, Mom, for your godly example!

As I mentioned before, there are different types of growth and stages of development that we experience in our life: physical, mental, career, social, and spiritual growth.

So, let's start with Jesus, our example and the author and finisher of our faith. Jesus was constantly advancing and progressing in His physical growth, as well as His spiritual growth, His social growth, His mental growth, and His assignment.

In Luke 2:52, it says:

> "And Jesus kept increasing in wisdom and stature, and in favor with God and men." (NASB)

Another translation of this same scripture says:

> "Meanwhile, Jesus kept on growing wiser and more mature, and in favor with God and his fellow man." (ISV)

According to this verse, Jesus kept increasing and growing in four areas:

1. In Wisdom
2. In Stature
3. In Favor with God His Father
4. In Favor with Man (Others)

Jesus continually increased and matured in wisdom, which was in concert with His physical growth. As He continued to grow physically, He also continued to grow in wisdom. Jesus' wisdom came from above, and that was part of the key to His success. He did not use earthly wisdom, which is earthly, sensual, and devilish, but relied on the pure wisdom from heaven.

> "But the wisdom from above is always pure, filled with peace, considerate and teachable. It is filled with love and never displays prejudice or hypocrisy in any form." (James 3:17 TPT)

Jesus continued to increase in stature. Stature can refer to someone's physical growth or to the high level of respect with which one is regarded, and Jesus grew in both. Of course, He continued growing physically, but also in integrity. Jesus made sure to take excellent care of His physical body because His body needed to be strong and healthy to accomplish His mission. He kept increasing in favor with His Father God as He grew in His spirituality and His relationship with His Father. He had an excellent relationship with His Father, and Jesus knew who He was and where He was going.

> *"Jesus told them, 'These claims are valid even though I make them about myself. For I know where I came from and where I am going, but you don't know this about me.'" (John 8:14 NLT)*

In Matthew 3:17, before Jesus officially began His ministry, He went down to the river Jordan and was baptized by His cousin John. Scripture says that after Jesus came out of the water, the heavens opened, and the Spirit of God descended like a dove and settled on Him. Then there was an audible voice from heaven that said, "This is My Beloved Son in whom I am well pleased." Through this act, God not only publicly endorsed and validated His Son, Jesus, and what He was sent to accomplish, but also said He was well pleased with Him.

There was also another time in the Gospels when God spoke audibly about His Son. This was during the time that Peter, James, and John were with Jesus during His transfiguration. God once again validated the fact that Jesus was favored and loved by Him.

> *"While he yet spake, behold, a bright cloud overshadowed them: and behold a voice out of the cloud, which said, This is my beloved Son, in whom I am well pleased; HEAR YE HIM." (Matthew 17:5 KJV)*

> *"For when he received honor and glory from God the Father, and the voice was borne to him by the Majestic Glory, 'This is my beloved Son, with whom I am well pleased, we ourselves heard this very voice borne from heaven, for we were with him on the holy mountain." (2 Peter 1:17-18 ESV)*

Jesus continued to grow in favor with Man and with others. His social and emotional development continuously grew. Jesus was so confident in who He was, He was able to confront the Sadducees and Pharisees by bringing to light their religious hypocrisy. Jesus knew how to answer every man. Though He was tempted on every hand, He overcame every temptation.

> *"So then, since we have a great High Priest who has entered heaven, Jesus the Son of God, let us hold firmly to what we believe." (Hebrews 4:14 NLT)*

> *"For we do not have a high priest who is unable to sympathize with our weaknesses. Instead, we have one who in every respect has been tempted as we are, yet he never sinned." (Hebrews 4:15 ISV)*

He moved with such compassion and love that it drew many people to Him, so much so that even the children wanted to stay in His presence. People flocked to hear Him break the Bread of Life and bring life to their souls by His teachings, signs, miracles, and wonders!

Jesus took the initiative and the responsibility to continue to grow in those four areas and, as a result, successfully completed His mission of saving us from our sins. So, if Jesus knew the importance of continual growth and development, then who are we to deny the fact that we need to do the same?

> *"And then our immaturity will end! And we will not be easily shaken by trouble, nor led astray by novel teachings or by the false doctrines of deceivers who teach clever lies But instead we will remain strong and always sincere*

> in our love as we express the truth. All our direction and ministries will flow from Christ and lead us deeper into him, the anointed Head of his body, the church." (Ephesians 4:1-15 TPT)

In this next section, let's delve into the different stages of spiritual growth and development and how they relate to the natural stages.

MUSING: THOUGHTS TO PROVOKE

"When you use Jesus as your example of spiritual growth and maturity, then you will experience an overflowing bountiful life that you could only previously imagine."
– Grace Blue

QUESTIONS TO PONDER:

How has the life of Christ caused you to reassess your own life to be more like Him? Are you willing to be more like Him? What changes are you going to make to assure that it happens?

THE "GESTER" OF GOD

> "Before I formed thee in the belly I knew thee; and before thou camest forth out of the womb I sanctified thee, and I ordained thee a prophet unto the nations." (Jeremiah 1:5 KJV)

The first stage of development is the conception and germination stage. In the natural, it's also called a time of gestation. It is the time between conception and birth when a baby is concealed inside its mother's womb, growing and developing. In the spiritual, you are hidden as you are being developed into the things of God.

"Gester" is the Greek word for this stage of maturation and its definition includes "fetus, womb, produced from seed."

When the egg and the sperm/seed unite together to form a new life, as *US NEWS & World Reports* stated in an article titled "During Conception, Human Eggs Emit Sparks," "an explosion of zinc fireworks occurs when a human egg is activated by a sperm enzyme. The intensity of the sparks, scientists say, indicates the egg's potential to develop into a healthy embryo." Scientist had seen the phenomenon occur in animals, but this was the first time it had also been shown to happen in human egg.

I call it an explosion or fireworks that occur when sperm/seed meets egg, which signals the beginning of life and fertilization occurs. I believe it's also the time when God detonates and activates purpose in us! I don't believe God waits until we are completely grown and get saved to ignite purpose in us. I believe that when that egg and sperm connect, purpose is ignited. Jeremiah was known, sanctified, and ordained by God as a Prophet of God before Jeremiah was formed in his mother's womb.

When fertilization occurs, the egg changes and closes shop so no other sperm can enter into the fertilized egg. At the moment of fertilization, the united egg and sperm merge and share their genetic material. The baby's sex and genes are set at this time. It is also at this time that the fertilized egg, the embryo, is implanted in the mother's womb and begins to multiply, grow, develop, and form the important bodily systems.

After the eighth week, the embryo is now called a fetus. The time the baby is in its mom's womb is an incubation period. Incubation is a time of maintaining controlled environmental conditions for the purpose of favorable growth and development of body organs, systems, and tissues. During this time of human gestation, you may not see much happening on the outside of the mother's body concerning the development of the fetus, but on the inside, so much is transpiring. During this time of being hidden away, many things are occurring in the baby's physical and mental development. But once a fetus gets to a certain level of growth, it begins to outgrow its environment. It becomes limited in what it can do or accomplish inside its mom's womb.

God has made our bodies, during this incubation process and period, to go from the very first time the egg and sperm connect and create a spark, to a whole person that is able to live and thrive outside of the womb environment. We are fearfully and wonderfully made by God. As complex as our human bodies are, I cannot imagine that there are people who do not believe that God is the Great Designer of our magnificent bodies. King David knew it quite well when he spoke about it in Psalm 139:

> *"Oh yes, you shaped me first inside, then out; you formed me in my mother's womb. I thank you, High God—you're breathtaking! Body and soul, I am marvelously made! I worship in adoration—what a creation! You know me inside and out, you know every bone in my body; You know exactly how I was made, bit by bit, how I was sculpted from*

nothing into something. Like an open book, you watched me grow from conception to birth; all the stages of my life were spread out before you, The days of my life all prepared before I'd even lived one day." (Psalm 139:13-16 The Message)

How does this miracle of gestation relate to spiritual growth and maturation? When you first come to Christ, a fire is ignited inside of you: a new beginning, newness of life. You're connected to God. You're no longer alienated with no known purpose – you wake up! Then you are hidden in Christ to develop further. This is the time when a person is refined and disciplined. If they're not careful, someone who comes to Christ can fizzle out during this time and become ineffective in God's fulfillment for their lives. They may even abort the relationship with the Father and fail to thrive.

The Parable of the Seed and the Sower, told by Jesus in Matthew 13:1-8, Mark 4:1-20, and Luke 8:4-15, is a good example of how someone can halt their development during the time they're hidden in the womb. Seed is planted by the farmer in different types of terrain with totally different results.

> *"That same day Jesus went out of the house and sat by the lake. Such large crowds gathered around him that he got into a boat and sat in it, while all the people stood on the shore. Then he told them many things in parables, saying: 'A farmer went out to sow his seed. As he was scattering the seed, some fell along the path, and the birds came and ate it up. Some fell on rocky places, where it did not have much soil. It sprang up quickly, because the soil was shallow. But when the sun came up, the plants were scorched, and they withered because they had no root. Other seed fell among thorns, which grew up*

> *and choked the plants. Still other seed fell on good soil, where it produced a crop—a hundred, sixty or thirty times what was sown. Whoever has ears, let them hear.'"*
> *(Matthew 13:1-9 NIV)*

Jesus explained this parable to His disciples when they inquired about its meaning. He said that the farmer who planted seeds on the footpath, which the birds came and ate, represented those who hear the message of the Kingdom but don't understand it, and because of that, the evil one comes and snatches away the seed that was planted in their hearts. It does not get a chance to go deep, germinate, and grow. There are too many believers who have come to Christ but end up having the Word stolen from them.

The seed on the rocky soil represents those who hear the Word and receive it joyously, but because the seed isn't given a chance to have deep roots, they don't last long. As soon as problems arise, or they are persecuted for believing God's Word, they fall away. They end up going back and doing the very same thing they were delivered from.

The seed that fell upon among the thorns, Jesus further explained to his disciples, represented those who hear God's Word but then become distracted from the Word by the cares of this life and the desire to obtain riches. As a result, there is no spiritual fruit that is produced because of those distractions.

> *"Do not love this world nor the things it offers you, for when you love the world, you do not have the love of the Father in you." (1 John 2:15 NLT)*

But Jesus further expressed that the seed that fell on good soil illustrated that those who truly hear and understand the Word of God activate it by producing a harvest that multiplies what has been planted in them. Continuous growth and development!

That's why it's important, once a person comes to Christ, to allow that Word of God inside them to germinate, incubate, and gestate while they are learning how to activate the Word of God. Allow the Word of God to grow deep so that when the person is birthed out of the incubation process, they will begin to bear fruit.

According to Tianna DuPont, "Viable seeds are living entities. They must contain living, healthy embryonic tissue in order to germinate. All fully developed seeds contain an embryo and, in most plant species, a store of food reserves, wrapped in a seed coat. Seeds generally 'wake up' and germinate when soil moisture and temperature conditions are correct for them to grow." The implication that Jesus gave in this parable was that in order for a seed to begin to germinate, the environment, moisture, and soil have to be conducive for growth.

The seed for us, Saints, is the Word of God, and we are the soil. The environment is our mind, will, and emotions, how we receive the Word, and the moisture is how we allow the Word of God to be activated in us. When it's time to be birthed out into the things of God, we must come forth ready to grow in His grace and in the knowledge of our Lord and Saviour Jesus Christ.

I believe that natural truths coincide with spiritual truths. Just as in the natural, the sperm or seed connects with the connect and sparks fly, so it is in the spiritual. When I got saved and received the Holy Spirit, the Holy Spirit and I connected in a mighty transforming way. Our connection produced a spark that started a fire in my soul. As I grow, develop, and mature in Christ, that spark turns into a blazing fire that burns away my sinful will, emotions, mind, and heart to be in complete alignment with Him and His will for me. Father, not my will be done, but your will be done on earth (in me), as it is in heaven (your perfect will for me). My desire is to align my will to His will. The way that can be done is through continuous growth and maturation. Just as Jesus was described in Luke 2:40-52, I have to keep on growing, keep on maturing in wisdom, by becoming strong in the Spirit, in favor with God and men so His grace, His favor, and spiritual blessings can continue to be upon me.

> *"...growing in every way more and more like Christ, who is the head of his body, the church."*
> *(Ephesians 4:15 NLT)*

Just as it is important to grow in the natural, so too is it important to grow spiritually. This period of incubation and germination can be viewed in other ways than just the process of receiving Jesus Christ as Lord and Saviour. For those of us who have received a prophetic word over the years, we are looking for the manifestation of that word. When we hear it, we are so overjoyed and often believe and hope it will manifest the next day, the next week, or even the next month, but instead, it feels like we're in a waiting pattern, like an airplane waiting to land that hasn't been given the clearance yet. But allow me to say that if it feels like nothing is happening with your prophetic word, you may be in a gestation stage. God may have you waiting in the womb of the prophecy until God finishes the work He needs to do concerning our character. If we want to have longevity in the area that God has spoken to us about, we must not jump out and help make it happen, but stay in the womb of God's prophetic word until we are birthed into it.

For example, if I've been given the prophetic word that I am to be a minister of the gospel, and that word of the Lord comes forth everywhere I go, if I'm not careful, I can become overly anxious that it's not happening quickly enough. I'm looking at the glitz and glamour of ministry (if there is such a thing), and it seems that neither my pastor nor the church leadership is recognizing the call of God on my life. So, I take matters into my own hands and go online and apply for ordination papers with an organization that I know nothing about. I'm not patient enough to wait on the Lord! Once those ordination papers come, I begin to go out and preach the gospel as an ordained minister and start my own ministry. My justification is that I just want to help God out and nobody understands what God has called me to do. I birth myself into ministry without allowing God to work out the necessary flaws in my life that would cause me to fizzle and burn out, and because of that, I have a failure to thrive. Many times, if we're birthed into ministry prematurely, it won't be long before our flaws will come to the surface.

But if I'm wise, I will wait on the timing of the Lord and allow Him to launch me forth. In my spiritual incubation period, I'm in a time of hiding while the Holy Spirit is helping me to put off the works of the flesh, clean up my act, and receive the necessary training in my gift and call so that when it's time for my birthing in ministry, I will have longevity. I must allow for that time of preparation. I need to develop in secret so that when the time of birthing into ministry happens, I will be ready! Even Jesus waited on the timing of God before He was birthed fully in ministry.

> *"But when the set time had fully come..."*
> *(Galatians 4:4 NIV)*

> *"Jesus was about thirty years old when he began his public ministry." (Luke 3:23 NLT)*

THE "NEPIOS" OF GOD

Now it's time for the baby to be birthed!

I'm the mother of four adult children, and I remember as soon as each one of my children was born, after the doctor made sure the baby's lungs were clear and that there were no problems, the doctor or the nurse would immediately put my baby on my chest or in my arms. They would also make sure my husband had an opportunity to hold the baby to develop that bonding. When I laid eyes on each one of my children and they were laid on my chest for the skin-to-skin touch, the feeling of love and joy was simply indescribable. It was that true connection or bond that transpired from my baby to me and from me to my baby.

According to Strong's Concordance, there are a few Greek words that describe this stage of development. One of these words is "tikto," which means to bring forth, a woman giving birth, to bear, to produce from a seed, to be born. Another is "brephos," which means infant, newborn child; it can sometimes refer to an unborn child. "Nepios" also applies to this stage of development, and it refers to an infant, little child, not speaking; babe, inexperienced; an immature Christian.

In this stage of development, one is no longer confined by the womb and its small space. There is only room for the baby and the placenta in the womb, but now it's time to be birthed into an unlimited space called the world. We can compare it to a fish tank: the fish can only grow as large as the tank, but if it's in the ocean, the fish's capacity to expand and grow is limitless.

> *"And she brought forth [tikto] her firstborn son, and wrapped him in swaddling clothes..." (Luke 2:7 KJV)*

Research has shown that a mother's breast milk is the purest milk that a baby can drink, especially if the mother is careful of what she eats. Breast milk provides nourishment and produces antibodies that help the baby's body fight off sickness and disease. Once the newborn latches on to a mother's breast for milk, they don't want any store-bought formula. Store-bought formula is just what it says, a formula that is filled with man's alternative to breast milk. Baby formula is counterfeit breast milk.

Just as a newborn baby desires the pure milk from their mother's breast, when a new believer in Jesus Christ begins to drink the pure milk of the Word of God, they don't want anything else. They don't want or need any man-made alternatives to the sincere milk of the Word of God. In the natural, when a baby is hungry, it cries out to be fed with milk; in the spiritual, the believer must cry out for the sincere milk of God's Word. This milk provides the proper nourishment that causes a believer to grow properly. Nothing can take the place of reading the Word of God. The Word of God acts as spiritual antibodies that fight off destructive spiritual invaders.

> *"In the same way that nursing infants [brephos] cry for milk, you must intensely crave the pure spiritual milk of God's Word. For this 'milk' will cause you to grow into maturity, fully nourished and strong for life—especially now that you have had a taste of the goodness of the Lord Jehovah and have experienced his kindness."* (1 Peter 2:2-3 TPT)

In this natural stage of development, the child is beginning to develop its gross motor skills of freely moving its arms and legs, scooting, crawling, walking, running, and climbing. The child is also developing its fine motor skills of finding small things on the floor and putting them in its mouth, learning to feed itself. Babies go from making sounds to babbling, to saying single words, and then to talking in sentences. A child in this stage of development goes from just drinking milk to finally eating solid food.

Also, in this stage of development, it is important that newborns bond with their parents. If they don't bond, a spirit of abandonment and a spirit of an orphan can develop into the baby. Spiritually, if the babe in Christ is not careful, they can remain in this stage of development and become more carnally minded than spiritually minded, and as a result, they are unable to continue to progress in their spiritual growth and development. That's why spiritual parents are so important in the spiritual maturation of a Believer.

> *"Brothers and sisters, when I was with you I found it impossible to speak to you as those who are spiritually mature people, for you are still dominated by the mind-set*

> *of the flesh. And because you are immature infants [nepios] in Christ, I had to nurse you and feed you with 'milk,' not with the solid food of more advanced teachings, because you weren't ready for it. In fact, you are still not ready to be fed solid food, for you are living your lives dominated by the mind-set of the flesh. Ask yourselves: Is there jealousy among you? Do you compare yourselves with others? Do you quarrel like children and end up taking sides? If so, this proves that you are living your lives centered on yourselves, dominated by the mind-set of the flesh, and behaving like unbelievers. For when you divide yourselves up in groups—a 'Paul group' and an 'Apollos group'—you're acting like people without the Spirit's influence."*
> (1 Corinthians 3:1-8 TPT)

In natural birth, after the mother gives birth to her child, the umbilical cord is clamped and cut from the navel. No longer is the fetus dependent upon the placenta for oxygen and nutrition. No longer is the fetus dependent on the limited growth space. It's time for the baby to be released from the confined space and take its first breath of air.

According to UC Davis Health, bonding is essential for normal infant development. When a parent consistently responds to an infant's needs, a trusting relationship and bonding takes place. This sets the stage for the growing child to enter lasting, healthy relationships with others throughout their life. If bonding does not take place, then there is a strong possibility that the child will grow up unable to develop healthy relationships, or they can develop a condition that psychologists call attachment disorder. This happens when a child has been abused or neglected, and it can result in difficulties in behavior and emotions. In the periodical Psychology Today, an article written by Tina Traster says that many adopted children, particularly from Russia and Eastern Europe, develop a behavior known as Reactive Attachment Disorder. These RAD babies have trouble attaching to their adoptive parents because they have been traumatized or neglected. This article described these children as not wanting to be held, not making eye contact; many do not even tolerate being held, nor do they relax in the warm, loving embrace of their parents. Scientists have learned that as a group, neglected or abandoned children tend to have abnormal circuitry in areas of the brain involved in parental bonding.

According to an article in the *London Journal of Primary Care*, the experiences a baby has with their caregivers will determine the early wiring and enabling of the millions and millions of new connections in the brain. Early bonding with caregivers is absolutely essential to the healthy development of the brain and the emotions.

The medical field understands the importance of bonding, especially in the first few days of a baby's life. So, they make sure that there is opportune time for bonding to take place by having the mom spend as much time as possible with the baby at the very beginning, because when bonding takes place, a child feels safe and secure. Skin to skin, mother to baby is important for the emotional well-being of the child, creating a warm, loving relationship so that a child can continue to thrive far into adulthood. The time when a mother and her newborn baby are skin to skin for an uninterrupted hour right after birth is known as the "Golden Hour," and many in the field of obstetrics are understanding the importance of this time with parents and the baby. Parents use this hour to speak words of encouragement, love, and acceptance. In this time, the baby is more apt to successfully latch on to the mother's breast for breastfeeding.

In the spiritual realm, if a child is rejected by a parent while in the womb or even after birth, a spirit of rejection can enter in and wreak havoc in the heart and mind of a child. It's a deep wound. A spirit of rejection can cause mental oppression through the form of loneliness, depression, and emotional scarring, among other things. If a baby is born and does not bond with a parent, then that spirit of rejection begins to form a mental stronghold around the child. That spirit of rejection constantly whispers in the child's ear that it is unloved and not accepted. That's why it's so important to accept and bond with your baby early on. It's important to validate and affirm a child early in their development.

The Word of God reminds us that once we come to Christ, we are accepted in the Beloved! He loves and cares for us. And as we are birthed and begin the spiritual growth process, bonding with God and with those He puts in our lives to shepherd and disciple us, we have a wonderful opportunity to have a healthy spiritual growth process. We are part of the Kingdom of God with all its rights and privileges. We have been adopted by Him, so instead of a spirit of rejection because of sin, we have a spirit of adoption. We know our Father God loves us and accepts us as His own, because we can feel His love and care!

> *"For you have not received a spirit of slavery leading to fear again, but you have received a spirit of adoption as sons by which we cry out, 'Abba! Father.'"* (Romans 8:15 NASB)

> "This Spirit of adoption that works in our lives is powerful; it is what infuses our lives with purpose, meaning and belonging." Cindi Trimm

In this "tikto" or birthing and the newborn "brephos" and "nepios" stage of development, it is vitally important to bond with our Spiritual Father God. Our Father has so lovingly invited us to bond with Him through the intimate and endearing title of "Abba." To us it's like using the word "Daddy." When my own adult children call their father Daddy, it's the sweetest sound. I know when I hear them call him Daddy, they are reinforcing the fact that they and their daddy have a close, endearing bond in their relationship with each other. Jesus used this endearing and intimate word to show the close love relationship He had with His Father in Mark 14:36a:

> "Abba, Father! All things are possible for You...." (Amplified Bible)

It is also important to bond with spiritual parents and mentors or those who can disciple. Spiritual parents are those God has directed to watch over you and help direct you in your spiritual development. Those who are mature enough to become spiritual parents must immediately connect with the new convert. During this period, spiritual parents must first make sure that the connection or bond with the new convert starts by bonding with their Father God. They must always point the new convert to Him. Over my years of pastoring, I've seen that in some cases, a person who brings someone to Christ feels that the new convert belongs to them. This breeds a relationship of control.

Cindi Trimm says that this is a time to have tutors and governors, as spoken about in Galatians 4:1-2. She says that tutors empower a person to build intellectual capacity, to maximize their potential. They are also a catalyst to aid in discovering a person's purpose. A governor, spoken of in Galatians 4, helps build social, cultural, and spiritual character. Governors hold you accountable morally and ethically. So, this stage of growth and development is a time to add more layers of assistance in our journey of spiritual maturation with mentors and those who are willing and able to disciple us.

> *"Now I say, That the heir, as long as he is a child [nepios], differeth nothing from a servant, though he be lord of all; But is under tutors and governors until the time appointed of the father. (Galatians 4:1-2 KJV)*

> *"Think of it this way. If a father dies and leaves an inheritance for his young children, those children are not much better off than slaves until they grow up, even though they actually own everything their father had. They have to obey their guardians until they reach whatever age their father set." (Galatians 4:1-2 NLT)*

The Apostle Paul understood the importance and the proper relationship of being a spiritual parent. He knew the importance of bonding with the heavenly Father, but he also understood that a godly sonship relationship was necessary for accountability and spiritual growth.

> *"For you may have countless instructors in Christ, but you don't have many fathers. For I became your father in Christ Jesus through the gospel. Therefore I urge you to imitate me. This is why I have sent Timothy to you.*

> *He is my dearly loved and faithful child in the Lord."*
> *(1 Corinthians 4:15-17 CSB)*

> *"To Titus, my true son in our common faith."*
> *(Titus 1:4 NIV)*

Paul was not bonded to Timothy and Titus biologically, so what was Paul's role as a spiritual father? It was to love them to greatness by leading, disciplining, nurturing, encouraging, and walking with them through trials and tribulations so that they would develop into manifest sons of God walking with God, in the power of God, and with the mind of Christ. A spiritual father or mother not only teaches and imparts identity, but also leads by example, providing steadfast love and wisdom to equip and empower their spiritual sons and daughters to move in the authority God has given them. Spiritual parents help lead their sons and daughters to spiritual maturity. This stage also allows the spiritual parent(s) to give the new babe in Christ the spiritual milk and foundation that's needed for them to grow spiritually healthy. Once they taste the milk of the Word of God, they will experience the goodness of the Lord and will want nothing else!

> *"Brothers, do not be children in your thinking. Be infants [nepiazo, taken from nepios] in evil, but in your thinking be mature." (1 Corinthians 14:20 ESV)*

That is why it's so important to bond with your spiritual parents as soon as you are birthed. Allow them to speak into your life, correct you, love you, and encourage you. And those who are mature enough must be willing to make the sacrifice of becoming spiritual parents. The Apostle Paul said in 1 Corinthians 11:1,

> *"Follow my example, as I follow the example of Christ."*
> *(NIV)*

It is important during this stage of development that a person not be left alone to fend for themself. At this stage of development, believers can easily be led astray because they are unwise in the Word. Mature leaders cannot allow believers at this stage to be tossed back and forth by deceitful teachers who can lead them astray. Instead, those who are mature and are considered mature teachers and leaders must pull them alongside and help them in their journey towards spiritual maturation. Spiritually mature believers who can provide a safe place are needed to teach those who are in this stage of development.

> *"That we henceforth be no more children [nepios], tossed to and fro, and carried about with every wind of doctrine, by the sleight of men, and cunning craftiness, whereby they lie in wait to deceive; But speaking the truth in love, may grow up into him in all things, which is the head, even Christ." (Ephesians 4:14-15 KJV)*

As I talked about before, I had a wonderful, loving biological mother who encouraged, uplifted, disciplined, and spoke words of affirmation to me. God also saw fit to bless me with a wonderful, powerful spiritual parent by the name of Bishop Patricia T. Whitelocke. Back when we first bonded with one another, I had never heard of spiritual parenting. I just knew that her inspiration and example was something that I needed and wanted. Bishop

Whitelocke is an amazing woman of God. She is the one who led me to Christ, introduced me to the workings of the Holy Spirit, challenged me to activate them in my life, and was responsible for my spiritual upbringing. This time of bonding with my spiritual parent was very crucial for me, because I believe that without the opportunity to bond with her, I would not have had the proper spiritual upbringing that God knew I needed for the leadership position I'm in today.

The nondenominational church that she co-founded and co-pastored was a dynamic ministry that was on the cutting edge. Not many ministries, especially African American ones, were having Christian summer camp for young people as well as adults in those days. Not only did we have fun and fellowship at summer camp, but we learned the Word of God. Not only did she teach us the Word of God, but she challenged us into activating the nine manifestations spoken of in 1 Corinthians 12. They were the most outstanding God-led weeks of the summer. She made sure that our camp experience was filled with the teaching and activation of the Word of God, developmentally appropriate activities, comfortable and affordable accommodations, and delicious meals.

One particular summer when Bishop Whitelocke did not have enough adult staff who would be able to attend camp, she decided to use the older youth and train them to be camp staff members and counselors. I was around 16 years old at the time, and of course, I happened to be one of the ones she trained. She took a chance with us young people, but she followed the leading of the Holy Spirit and saw us through the Spirit's lens. She saw greatness in us and saw us as God saw us. As a result of her taking that chance with us, many who heeded the call are today preachers, teachers, deacons and deaconesses, pastors, prophets, and evangelists, solid in our walk with the Lord. She was a dynamic radio and television host broadcasting in multiple cities. She is an innovator, motivator, an emancipator, and an activator. She is truly a visionary. God Bless Bishop Patricia T. Whitelocke!

> **QUESTIONS TO PONDER:**
>
> Who have you bonded with who have become your spiritual parents? How's it working for you?

THE "PAIDION" OF GOD

I remember when my children were in the infant/toddler stage of development, they were so cute and innocent. I loved watching them first realize they had hands and fingers as they explored their bodies and began to recognize their surroundings. As they learned to talk and walk, it was so cute and fun to watch and experience. What a joy I had as a parent to witness the various changes of growth and development my children went through as toddlers. It was beautiful seeing their personalities develop. Four children, four different personalities. I also remember that during this stage of development, I could not leave them alone unless they were in the bed asleep. Even then, my husband and I still had to peek in on them to make sure they were sleeping, because they would sometimes get up and become so busy exploring their surroundings. They were so excited about everything around them, and as a result, they were not aware of things that were dangerous to them as they explored. That's why they needed strict supervision from us as their parents. It was necessary for us to teach them what was good for them and what would do them harm. During this stage of development, my husband and I made sure we showered them with much love, affection, and affirmation. Oh, how we love each one of our babies!

As we move to this next stage of spiritual maturation, you will really understand the importance of having spiritual parents. Children need parents to oversee their growth and development as well as being their caregivers. In the natural, this toddler and preschool stage comes between two and six years of age. In the same stage of spiritual development, a new believer in Christ experiences true freedom in God and begins to flex their curiosity about the things of God.

According to Erik Erikson's stages of psychosocial development, children in this stage of development are learning to be self-sufficient, and their imagination is in full swing. They are learning to relate to others and developing a better understanding of who they are as individuals. This is a stage where affirmation is needed, as well as supervision. In this stage of development, there is quite a bit of interaction. According to an article in *Scholastic Parents*, most of a child's social and emotional growth occurs in the relationship with caregivers.

A child in this stage of development needs loving parents who are very attentive and supportive, as the child is solely dependent upon their caregivers for their well-being. This attentiveness and support generally includes affirming them by smiling at them, giving them words of encouragement and affirmation, celebrating their successes, and showing interest in what interests them, to name a few. A child needs to know they are loved, valued, special, and important to their parent(s). This is done by the positive ways in which parents react and respond to their child.

This stage of development is a time of teaching a child self-control. In the natural, one of the ways a child is taught self-control is by being potty trained. I remember trying to potty train my children. It was at times very frustrating, but it was also rewarding, especially when they made it to the toilet in time and didn't soil their clothes. I certainly knew it was time to potty train them when they took off their soiled diaper and brought it to me and said "nasty."

Self-control is one of the nine fruits of the Spirit spoken of in Galatians 5:22-26. The previous verses (5:19-21) speak about the works of the flesh, which are diametrically opposed to the will and righteousness of God. The works of the flesh equate to self-indulgence and a lack of self-control. The end result breeds self-destruction.

In Strong's Concordance, the Greek word "paidion" is the closest word to describe this stage, and it refers to an "infant, young child, little one." During this "paidion" stage of maturation, one is exercising and operating in their own self-will: the will to do what they want, when they want. This is a time when parents teach their child the necessity of submitting to their authority for their own protection. If a parent isn't careful, while the child is exercising their will to have it their way, the parent can give in, especially if the child has a temper tantrum. The tendency can be to allow the child to have its way so the parent can have peace of mind. But if the parents do give in, the child will have a difficult time in life submitting to authority. You will find that in all of the stages of spiritual growth and maturity, submission is a major factor and focus.

A new believer in Christ Jesus is so excited about their new freedom in Him. They feel so free and uninhibited in the Spirit that they sometimes venture too far outside the will of God for their lives. During this stage of spiritual maturation, a person is learning submission to God and to their spiritual parents. In fact, part of spiritual parenting is the responsibility to teach the importance of submitting their will to God's will for their lives. This submission is not control or oppression; it's to foster a right relationship with God and those He assigned to help develop you. In fact, the word *submission* in the New Testament comes from the Greek word "hupotasso," which, according to the NAS New Testament Lexicon, is a military term which means "to arrange (troop divisions) in a military fashion under the command of a leader. In non-military use, it is "a voluntary attitude of giving in; cooperating."

In his book *Sparkling* Gems, Rick Renner uses the word "hupotasso" to describe an individual who willfully places himself back under command. Renner says that this word signifies that a person has "willfully arranged himself under his commanding officer."

> *"Submit [hupotasso] yourselves therefore to God. Resist the devil, and he will flee from you." (James 4:7 KJV)*

According to this definition of *submit,* the Apostle James is encouraging us as believers to willfully put ourselves under the authority of God so that we'll be able to know when the devil is attempting to entrap us. Instead of the intended entrapment, we are able to resist him, and he has to retreat. He has to vamoose!

Previously, we spoke about how Jesus continuously grew spiritually, physically, socially, and with wisdom according to Luke 2:52. John the Baptist had the same experience with his continuous growth to fulfill the assignment that God had given him at his conception.

> *"And the child [paidion] grew [continued to grow] and became strong in spirit; and he lived in the wilderness until he appeared publicly to Israel." (Luke 1:80 NIV)*

In Matthew 18, Jesus says that if we want to enter the Kingdom, we must be as little children (paidion). He didn't mean we were to be childish, but childlike. We must come into the Kingdom as children, eager to learn, and have a heart that wants to grow and develop to know more about the ways of the Kingdom of God. This is a time to learn how to renew our minds, according to Romans 12:2.

Jesus even used the term "paidion" when he talked to His disciples after His resurrection. Even though the disciples had been in the presence of Jesus after His resurrection, they did not discern the power of His resurrection and what it encompassed, so they decided to go back to their old fishing place, to their old ways of fishing. They were comfortable in their old routines, even though they were not productive. Jesus challenged them to change directions. He referred to them as little children and redirected them to try fishing on the other side of their boat. When the disciples obeyed Jesus and let down their net, lo and behold, they had so many fish they couldn't even pull them up into the boat.

> *"Then Jesus saith unto them, Children [paidion], have ye any meat? They answered him, No. And he said unto them, Cast the net on the right side of the ship, and ye shall find. They cast therefore, and now they were not able to draw it for the multitude of fishes." (John 21:5-6 KJV)*

I believe Jesus tested them to see if they would change course if He asked them to, and because they did, they were the recipients of an abundance of blessings. Because of their obedience to the voice of Jesus, the disciples reaped a harvest.

The Apostle Paul instructs us as believers not to be children in our thinking:

> *"Brothers, do not be children [paidion] in your thinking. Be infants in evil, but in your thinking be mature." (1 Corinthians 14:20 ESV)*

In the spiritual, this stage of growth and development requires a great deal of supervision. Submission is still a major factor in moving from this stage of spiritual development to the next. Those in this stage are still led by the flesh: they are still carnal.

If godly character isn't developed during this time, it can result in arrested development. Some of you may ask, "What is arrested development?" According to Collins Dictionary, it is a psychological development that is not complete. The word *arrested* means "to bring to a stop, to slow; to make inactive, seize capture, to take or keep in custody by authority of the law." So, arrested development is growth that is stagnated, put in custody (by that which has the authority to do so), which slows down or stops growth. Arrested development can affect body, soul, and spirit.

In the body, arrested development can slow down or stop physical growth, which can include stunted motor skills, muscular dystrophy, and the like. Arrested development can also affect the soul, which includes the mind, will, and emotions. The mind can be affected by impulsivity, fears, insecurities, confusion, learning disabilities, and short attention span. There can be a strong self-will resulting in rebelliousness and tantrums. The emotions can be affected by overdependence on others, doublemindedness, and frustration. In the spiritual, arrested development can retard spiritual growth and development, causing such problems as faulty judgment and discernment, misunderstanding of scriptures, false doctrine, error and heresy, guilt, and condemnation.

Suppose we have spiritual leaders that have arrested development! That can cause those they lead to be stunted in their spiritual growth as well. That's why it's important that we have mature leaders leading the flock of God. There have been situations and circumstances that occur because leaders who have not grown up and grown deep in God lead the sheep, those they have been entrusted with, down the path of destruction. They can pass on their own insecurities, doubt, frustration, rebelliousness, and doublemindedness onto those they supposedly have care over.

Again, as in the previous stages, great supervision on the part of spiritual parent(s) is crucial, because this is a time when guidance into godly character and integrity is being developed into the life of a believer. Godly character isn't just something that you show people; it is etched in a person's heart based upon their relationship with God and the studying of His Word. It's what we learn when we have challenges, and it turns into our reason for doing what we do, because we are relying on our relationship with our Father God and the understanding and activation of the Word of God in our lives. Character becomes our motivation for our actions. It's the "why"! Character is our moral compass, and integrity is the living out of that moral code. It's what we do and say when no one is around. This is a time when a Believer grows in intimacy with the Father, grows in His strength, His wisdom, and His love! This is when a person in this stage begins to experience the Kingdom of the Father.

> *"For we are his workmanship, created in Christ Jesus for good works, which God prepared beforehand that we should walk in them." (Ephesians 2:10 ESV)*

> *"For we are God's masterpiece. He has created us anew in Christ Jesus, so we can do the good things he planned for us long ago." (Ephesians 2:10 NLT)*

MUSING: THOUGHTS TO PROVOKE

"Spiritual immaturity stops you from being closer to God, and if you don't make the choice to change, it doesn't matter whether you hang out with Christians, talk about God all day long, attend church every Sunday or listen to sermons every day, you won't change. The choice is yours, and no one else will make it for you."
– Benita Vaye/United Generation

QUESTIONS TO PONDER:

How have you submitted to God and your spiritual parents so you can grow with grace? Are you desiring the sincere milk of the Word of God by reading and ingesting it, so you can grow into the full experience of your salvation?

CHAPTER 5:
DEVELOPMENTAL STAGES OF SPIRITUAL GROWTH

THE "PAIS" OF GOD

We're calling the next stage of spiritual growth and development the "pais" stage. "Pais" is a Greek word, and according to the Biblical Greek Primer by Bill Mounce, it means "boy, child, youth, usually below the age of puberty and not necessarily male; a personal servant, attendant; a child, in relation to parents, of either sex." This stage can be between the ages of 7 to 12 years.

> *"And Jesus rebuked the demon, and it came out of him, and the boy [pais] was healed instantly."*
> *(Matthew 17:18 ESV)*

> *"And when they had fulfilled the days, as they returned, the child [pais] Jesus tarried behind in Jerusalem; and Joseph and his mother knew not of it."* *(Luke 2:43 KJV)*

According to Ariba Khaliq, children from age 7 to 12 are in the time of transformation, which Khaliq calls the middle childhood years. There are physical, intellectual and emotional changes. If parents are really diligent during this stage, they can help their child mature into a responsible person. During this physical stage of development, a person has more self-regulation skills. They go from completely depending upon their parents to achieving a level of independence. They are more aware of right and wrong, whether they adhere to it or not. Khaliq also mentions in her article that children in this stage are mature enough to control their emotions, but they are also more peer-conscious and gravitate more towards peer relationships rather than parental. They will go from playing alone to playing and interacting with their peers. Friendships are more important to them at this stage of development. Physically, children in this stage are at the onset of their puberty years.

How does this relate to spiritual maturation? As with the previous stages of maturation, a person still needs a great deal of supervision. Spiritual parents, mentors, those who can disciple are still as important in this stage as in the earlier stages. One cannot jump over this stage to the next one, just as you can't jump over a stage of physical development. The way God has designed the body and mind, you have to go through this growth stage. It is important that a person is discipled, because discipline is so important. This is a time to renew the mind, and transformation should take place as we continue our journey to spiritual growth and maturity.

> *"And do not be conformed to this world, but be transformed by the renewing of your mind, that you may prove what is that good and acceptable and perfect will of God."* (Romans 12:2 NKJV)

> *"And do not be conformed to this world [any longer with its superficial values and customs], but be transformed and progressively changed [as you mature spiritually] by the renewing of your mind [focusing on godly values*

> *and ethical attitudes], so that you may prove [for yourselves] what the will of God is, that which is good and acceptable and perfect [in His plan and purpose for you]."*
> *(Romans 12:2 Amplified Bible)*

At this crucial stage of maturation, the emphasis should be on teaching the believer how to discipline their mind, refine their temperament, and control their emotions by being doers of the Word of God and not allowing the mind to resist. Mentally resisting is called passive aggression.

A leader may ask a believer to complete a task because they are trying to help disciple them, or to help build their capacity and character so that the call of God on their lives would have longevity. The believer may agree to do it, if perhaps reluctantly, but in their heart, mind, and actions, they don't agree, and because of that, they will not give their all to the cause of Christ. They may complete the task slowly or inefficiently, and this passive aggression is often done to maintain a level of independence.

Passive aggression may show up in various ways. According to the Seattle Christian Counseling website, passive aggressiveness can take on many forms, but each one can germinate into negative behavior. It happens when a person expresses their negative emotions indirectly. So, instead of being assertive and communicating honestly, a person may resist someone else's demands or expectations either by procrastinating, evading problems or issues, sulking, obstructing, or deliberately stalling or preventing an event or change. God has given us authority over our emotions. That's why it's so important to have spiritual parents and even peers who are genuinely committed to helping you grow spiritually.

During the time when my own children were between the ages of 7 to 12, their dad and I would ask them to complete a specific task like make up their bed or clean their room. They would reluctantly agree to do it, but when we checked on their progress, the bed was half made and the room was not cleaned. Now, mind you, they knew how to clean a room effectively and make a bed correctly. But by not doing it to the extent we expected them to, they maintained a level of independence. This was truly unacceptable to us as their parents. So, of course, we had them go back and complete their task as requested. As parents, we have to learn to use wisdom and allow our children to express their discontent with respect, but still expect them to complete tasks thoroughly, because through this, they will learn the importance of completion with excellence.

It's important that spiritual parents and those who are discipling a person not allow them to get away with anything that will allow negativity to set in. Submission and cooperation to authority is key to spiritual maturation. If one is to be great in the Kingdom of God, Jesus said, you must serve. This stage of development is a time to humble ourselves and submit to the will and purposes of God. Even Jesus, with all the power and authority He possessed and manifested, submitted to the will of His Father. An example of Jesus' submission was when He was in the garden of Gethsemane before starting the process of sacrificing His life for mankind.

> *"Father, if you are willing, please take this cup of suffering away from me. Yet I want your will to be done, not mine."*
> *(Luke 22:42 NLT)*

A believer can be tempted to spiritually wander, especially if they don't submit to the people God has put in their lives to aid in their maturation. This can stifle a believer's spiritual growth and development if they don't have any roots anywhere because they don't want to submit and be committed to anyone who can help them mature. In this stage, a person has to be careful not to allow their emotions and self-will to have preeminence.

Over the years, I've seen people church hop under the guise, in some cases, of calling it church hurt. Mind you, I am not minimizing church hurt, because that is real. But in reality, people have used that excuse and others to move from church to church because they are unwilling to submit, commit, or allow accountability in their life. I've found that there is a segment of Believers who don't realize that their unwillingness to change is stunting and stagnating their spiritual growth and maturity. They don't want anyone appearing to tell them what to do, because they want to maintain their complete independence, or the issue may be that they have an indiscretion, and the leader has brought it to their attention and wants to help them be an overcomer. What they may not realize is that they are also becoming independent of God. This is a time when God wants us to really buckle down, go past our negative feelings and emotions, and collaborate with the Holy Spirit in our own spiritual growth and development.

In the natural, we can't really imagine a child between the ages of 7 to 12 deciding they don't want to live with their parents anymore because they didn't like or agree with their rules and didn't want to submit to their authority, then going to live with another family and finding that they didn't like their rules and didn't want to submit to their authority either, then leaving that family and going to live with yet another family. You and I both know that none of those shenanigans would be tolerated in a child. So, why do we tolerate it when it comes to spiritual development?

The devil wants to move us out of the place of greatness. He does that by attempting to convince us to rely on our emotions and feelings, what others think or say, and our insecurities in order to dictate to us the direction we should go, instead of listening to what our Father God has purposed for us. Many times, if they are not careful, the Pais of God can cause discord in a fellowship of believers if they are not able to forgive those they feel have sinned against them. But, if we are wise during this stage of maturation, we will trust and rely on our spiritual parents, mentors, those who disciple us, the Holy Spirit, the Word of God, the Five-Fold Ministry, and His Grace to see us through the process. We must willingly submit to their authority and guidance. Let us trust God and not resist as we move through the process of spiritual maturation. 2 Peter 1:5-8 sums up the process:

> *"...make every effort to supplement your faith with virtue, and virtue with knowledge, and knowledge with self-control, and self-control with steadfastness, and steadfastness with godliness, and godliness with brotherly affection, and brotherly affection with love. For if these qualities are yours and are increasing, they keep you from being ineffective or unfruitful in the knowledge of our Lord Jesus Christ." (ESV)*

> **MUSING: THOUGHTS TO PROVOKE**
>
> "Here's one of my favorite statements: We are never going to enjoy stability, we are never going to enjoy spiritual maturity until we learn how to do what's right when it feels wrong, and every time you do what's right by a decision of your will using discipline and self control to go beyond how you feel, the more painful it is in your flesh, the more you're growing spiritually at that particular moment." – Joyce Meyer
>
> **QUESTIONS TO PONDER:**
>
> How are you doing with submitting to spiritual authority? What challenges and/or victories are you having with it?

THE "TEKNON" OF GOD

The next stage of spiritual maturation is the "teknon" stage between the ages of 12 and 20, which is considered the age of adolescence. This is a time after the onset of puberty when a person is between childhood and adulthood. Puberty is the changes that take place in a person's body to make them capable of reproduction. We also call this time period the teenage years. Many physical, emotional, behavioral, and social changes occur in the lives of those going through this stage of maturation. They increasingly prefer spending time with their friends than with the adults in their lives. They are inclined to be in control, define who they are, go their own way, and do their own thing. The textbook *Sociology, the Study of Human*

Society identifies five leading characteristics of the adolescent: biological growth and development, an undefined status, increased decision making, increased pressures, and the search for self.

There are so many changes taking place during adolescence. Growth spurts, voice changes, and the development of sexual characteristics all fall under biological growth and development. During this stage of growth and maturation, more decision making is made and peer pressure is predominant. They want more and more independence, whether they're ready for it or not. In the age of social media and the internet, they are exposed to so much and, in many cases, too soon. Social media has had an impact on teens' worldviews, both positive and negative.

As my own children transitioned into the adolescent years, there was a big difference in their attitude, their ideology, their worldview, and how they viewed us as their parents. They went from thinking that my husband and I knew everything to thinking we knew absolutely nothing. Their friends became the center of their lives. I loved the independence they projected, but as parents, we had to still have oversight over them, because they didn't know as much about life as they thought they did. The temptation for adolescents is to resist submitting to their parents' authority. Like many others their age, my children were tempted and succumbed to rebellion against our authority. This was a time when they could and did make some dumb decisions, as we have all done during this stage of development. Parents and the mature adults in their lives were crucial during this time, because the mistakes they could possibly make could haunt them for the rest of their lives. As parents, we were busy making sure that they were fed spiritually, challenged mentally, and involved in activities that would result in their betterment.

In this stage of spiritual maturation, the level of authority given by God is probationary. He needs to know if He can trust you. This puts a person in the position of needing to have a mentor or one who disciples them as a guide or a counselor. In the natural, during the time of adolescence and puberty, a person has everything they need in their bodies to produce children, but they are not mature enough to do so, either mentally or emotionally. In the spiritual, a person has the capabilities to become a mother or father in the Lord, but in this stage of development, it's not the time to parent or mentor anyone. It's too early! You still have a lot to learn and experience.

Teens, in the natural, have a tendency not to want accountability, not to want to be disciplined or corrected. They tend to want their own way, and as a result, they may move into rebellion if they're not careful. In the spiritual, the same thing can occur. So, having accountability, submitting to authority, and discipline are all so important. This is a very important stage of maturation because it requires spiritual parents and mentors to help the believer to become focused, especially in the areas of their giftings, talents, and calling. This is the time when they are trained in their calling and in what it means to follow Christ. The first submission needs to be to God. It is during this "teknon" stage of maturation that a Believer comes to a realization, actualization, and acknowledgement of God as their Father.

DEVELOPMENTAL STAGES OF SPIRITUAL GROWTH

> *"Behold what manner of love the Father has bestowed on us, that we should be called children [teknon] of God! Therefore, the world does not know us, because it did not know Him." (1 John 3:1 NKJV)*

God is positioning you for the world to see you as a Son of God. Like the Jewish bar/bat mitzvah, this is a time for a Believer's rite of passage. This is the time for independence under authority and with limited authority. A Believer in this stage of development needs to deliberately submit themselves to God and to their spiritual parents and mentors in order for that rite of passage to take place. I always say that one of the greatest abilities that God has given us is the ability to make choices.

> *"...My son, do not despise the chastening of the LORD, Nor be discouraged when you are rebuked by Him." (Hebrews 12:5 NKJV)*

Chastening in this verse is from the Greek word "paideia," which means "to teach, to train; to train children, or anyone, with strict discipline to help them mature and become responsible adults; to assist one in reaching full potential." God is using this time to teach, train, and develop a Believer to walk in spiritual maturity. As He teaches us, our responsibility is to self-correct and to renew our minds.

You have to position yourself as a student. This is when the person you submit to recognizes your gifts, talents, and calling, and they begin the process of helping to direct you there. You are being corrected or disciplined because the ultimate goal is to help you build and expand your capacity to carry the glory and presence of God in your life. Even though it doesn't feel good when you are disciplined, you must trust your mentor. Your mentor and/or spiritual parents must be given the spiritual responsibility by God, and they must possess the spiritual maturity to help build and expand capacity in you.

Decision making won't be taken from you. Your mentor and spiritual parents, along with God, will begin to discipline and test your decision making and your character. That's what they're there for. We must have people in our lives, especially during this stage of maturation, to challenge our thinking and our actions to make sure our choices for the direction we are taking are in full alignment with God's will, purpose, and plan for our lives.

> *"The Spirit himself testifies with our spirit that we are God's children [teknon]." (Romans 8:16 BSB)*

We must not compromise our Christian values, even though the temptation to do so is there. If we do, then we are behaving like the "teknon" of the devil. This is the time in our spiritual maturation when we are questioned on whether or not we are sacrificing God's will for our own will. It is said that during this stage, the children of God will be distinguished from the children of the devil based upon our righteous walk with God.

> *"By this the children [teknon] of God are distinguished from the children [teknon] of the devil: Anyone who does not practice righteousness is not of God, nor is anyone who does not love his brother." (1 John 3:10 BSB)*

Even the Apostle Paul was agonizing over the "teknon" Believers in the Galatian church. He said he was going to agonize over them, as if he were having labor pains, until Christ was formed in their hearts. He was going to labor with them until they became more like Christ. When you have those in your life who care about your spiritual growth to the point that they spend their time helping to grow you up, you know that's love!

> *"You are my dear children, but I agonize in spiritual 'labor pains' once again, until the Anointed One will be fully formed in your hearts!" (Galatians 4:19 TPT)*

We must continue to access our walk with the Lord to make sure we are aligned with His Word, His Will, His Way. This is a time in our maturation when we learn to become overcomers and walk in an overcoming attitude and action. This stage, if done properly, will prepare a believer to be an effective parent and mentor to others, reproducing in others what has been produced in them.

> *"Ye are of God, little children [teknon], and have overcome them: because greater is he that is in you, than he that is in the world." (1 John 4:4 KJV)*

QUESTIONS TO PONDER:

In what ways are you showing your accountability to God and those that God has put in your life to mentor/disciple you?

THE "NEANISKOS" OF GOD

In this stage of spiritual maturation, you have a young woman or man who has successfully survived the "teknon" stage. Hurray! We're calling this stage of growth and development the "neaniskos" stage, and it comes between the ages of 20 and 30. "Neaniskos" is a Greek word meaning "a youth, young man, under 40; used of a young attendant or servant."

In the natural, a young man or woman has moved from the teen years into the adult stage of development. One characteristic of this stage is the further development of their critical thinking skills. Generally, their relationships are formed based upon the values and beliefs they share. They have a better hold on their emotions and don't allow them to control their decisions – at least, I must add, in most cases! Also, they're not constrained by family or school as they were in their teen years. They are considered adults, and most behave as such by taking on the responsibility of an adult. They're strong, adventuresome, generally healthy, and ready to conquer the world. Because they're young, in most cases they are not afraid to tackle the challenges that come their way with the attitude that they can overcome any challenge.

In this stage of spiritual development, the young man or woman has learned to walk in the overcoming power of Jesus Christ. They are no longer children but have matured and learned how to overcome the "evil one" without backing down. Reaching this stage of spiritual maturation indicates that they have suffered and, through the suffering, have become an overcomer.

DEVELOPMENTAL STAGES OF SPIRITUAL GROWTH

In 1 John 2:13-14, the Apostle John encourages those in the different stages of maturity. For each level of maturity, he relates to them with what they have accomplished.

> *"I remind you, fathers and mothers [pater]: you have a relationship with the One who has existed from the beginning. And I remind you, young people [neaniskos]: you have defeated the Evil One. I write these things to you, dear children [paidion], because you truly have a relationship with the Father. I write these things, fathers and mothers [pater], because you have had a true relationship with him who is from the beginning. And I write these things, young people [neaniskos], because you are strong, the Word of God is treasured in your hearts, and you have defeated the Evil One." (TPT)*

There is nothing like having a level of maturity with experience under your belt. The Neaniskos of God has a spiritual strength that is exhibited consistently throughout the believer's life. It has become a lifestyle with an overcoming mindset.

I was recently listening to an interview with a medical doctor, who is also a pastor. She had been persecuted relentlessly based upon very unpopular statements she made concerning a medication that was rejected by others in the medical field. There were other doctors with her who spoke the same message in public as she did. In fact, they stood as a united front. But the media focused on the female doctor, whose origin happened to be from another country, and who was a pastor and a deliverance minister. The media started focusing on her and her ministry by pulling up her sermons concerning demon possession and deliverance from demons. Major news media lambasted her and made fun of her by implying that she was crazy and calling her a quack. The interviewer asked her if she felt vilified. She responded by saying it did not bother her, that she was God's battle ax and that her ministry has the fire of the Holy Spirit! She also said that the news media that tried to vilify her has instead become a boom to her ministry and medical practice. Instead of the devil trying to defeat and shame her, she took the opportunity to look at her situation as a victorious moment. She rose up in God's strength, defeated the evil one with the Word of God, and received the victory.

In spite of the obstacles faced, a believer in this stage of maturity consistently has a victorious mindset and walks in victory. They do not give up or cave in to adversity; they stand firm on the promises and authority of God!

In this stage of maturation, the young man or woman sees, understands, and walks confidently in their purpose. They are focused less on themselves and more on others. Even though they have a servant's heart, however, they are not necessarily strategic in the training of others. Those in this stage of maturation still need spiritual parents, mentors, and those who can disciple them and continue to direct them in the call of God on their lives. Even with their boldness and courage, they are still in need of encouragement and accountability, because they can easily stray into areas that God has not called them to spiritually tackle. An example of this is in Acts 7: when Stephen was being stoned, Saul, who later became the Apostle Paul, thought he was doing God a favor by persecuting Christians. Notice that he was in the "neaniskos" stage of development at that time of his life.

> "And cast him [Stephen] out of the city, and stoned him: and the witnesses laid down their clothes at a young man's [neaniskos] feet, whose name was Saul."
> (Acts 7:58 KJV)

In the "neaniskos" stage of maturation, a Believer is really understanding and beginning to walk in the purposes of God.

THE "HUIOS" OF GOD

This is a wonderful and amazing stage of spiritual maturation: the unveiling of the fully mature, Christ-like son of God. The Greek word "huios" is described as "mature sons or daughters, a son by birth or adoption; sharing the same nature as their Father, resembling their father; a true follower." This word is also used to describe the position given or recognized in a family with the same authority as the other adults in the family.

In Matthew 3, when Jesus was about to begin His ministry, His Father affirmed Jesus after He was baptized, using the word "huios" for Son, and God also affirmed Jesus as His Son during the transfiguration.

> "This is my beloved Son [huios], in whom I am well pleased." (Matthew 3:17 KJV)

> "Then the voice of God thundered from within the cloud, 'This is my Son, my Beloved One. Listen carefully to all he has to say.'" (Luke 9:35 TPT)

This word "huios" represents the fully developed, fully matured son or daughter who knows their place and position in the Body of Christ and serves in it. 1 Corinthians 12:18 says that God places each one in the Body of Christ where they fit and will function. The Huios of God no longer needs a guardian but walks securely in their position as a son and knows their rights and privileges as a son or daughter. They are neither intimidated by nor trying to be like anyone else, but they are secure in the knowledge and operation of their gifts, talents, and calling. They know their purpose because they know who they are and why they are here. They move with confidence in the power and authority that was given on the day of Pentecost.

The Huios of God knows that whatever they do and wherever they go, they represent their Father God! On purpose, they are looking and acting more and more like their Father, because they are very aware that they are carrying His glory.

The intimacy they have with the Father is precious because they are spending more time with Him and getting to know Him better and better. They are becoming a true Ambassador for Christ, sent by the Father to reconcile the world back to Him. A person in this stage of spiritual maturity, the Huios of God, knows that they have been entrusted with the Gospel of Jesus Christ and that it is important for them to flow in that authority with righteousness and holiness.

The Huios of God is no longer sin conscious but righteous conscious. The practice of sin is behind them. It doesn't mean that they don't sin, but it means that when they do, they know that they can ask for forgiveness and that God is faithful and just to forgive us of sin and cleanse us from all unrighteousness, according to 1 John 1:9. Their consistent focus is on their close relationship with the Father and how to better please Him and live in holiness. They are walking in the spirit of God, and it's evident through the production of the fruit of the Spirit spoken of in Galatians 5:22-24, as opposed to the works of the flesh spoken of in Galatians 5:19-21. Hypocrisy is not a part of their DNA. They are following the leading of the Holy Spirit.

> *"The mature children [huios] of God are those who are moved by the impulses of the Holy Spirit." (Romans 8:14 TPT)*

The Huios of God knows that they are not perfect but that the perfect one lives inside of them, and because of that, they are very aware of their walk in Christ. They want to make sure they are living the life of righteousness and holiness. They understand that because of Jesus' sacrifice, their standing in God is that they're righteous and holy. But they also align their state with their standing in God. They are walking in love and forgiveness. Knowing they are still in a spiritual battle of the flesh against the spirit, they do not take it lightly. They don't make excuses or cover up the sins they may commit. The Huios of God knows how to freely go to the throne of grace and get help in the time of need. They are aware of the realness of their enemy, the devil, and because of that, they are careful to keep on the whole armor of God, as spoken of in Ephesians 6.

The Huios of God manifests as a true son or daughter of God by walking fully in the power and authority of the Holy Spirit without hesitation. They are steadfast, immovable, always abounding in the work of the Lord, for they know their labor is not in vain.

In this stage of spiritual maturation, the Huios of God understands the importance of the correction of God that is given through the Holy Spirit, the Word of God, mentors/disciplers, the Five-Fold Ministry, and His Grace. In the earlier stages of development, submission is an area where each one has to learn to yield, but the Huios of God readily yields to spiritual authority.

They know, during times of tribulation, pain, and trouble, where to go and get uplifted and encouraged. They are not fighting the same battles or going through the same cycles. They know they are overcomers, and those around them see them as great examples of how a son or daughter of God, a Huios of God, ought to behave.

> *"So consider carefully how Jesus faced such intense opposition from sinners who opposed their own souls, so that you won't become worn down and cave in under life's pressures. After all, you have not yet reached the point of sweating blood in your opposition to sin. And have you forgotten his encouraging words spoken to you as his children? He said, 'My child, don't underestimate the value of the discipline and training of the Lord God, or get depressed when he has to correct you. For the Lord's training of your life is the evidence of his faithful love. And when he draws you to himself, it proves you are his delightful child.' Fully embrace God's correction as part of your training, for he is doing what any loving father does for his children. For who has ever heard of a child who never had to be corrected? We all should welcome*

> *God's discipline as the validation of authentic sonship. For if we have never once endured his correction it only proves we are strangers and not sons. And isn't it true that we respect our earthly fathers even though they corrected and disciplined us? Then we should demonstrate an even greater respect for God, our spiritual Father, as we submit to his life-giving discipline. Our parents corrected us for the short time of our childhood as it seemed good to them. But God corrects us throughout our lives for our own good, giving us an invitation to share his holiness. Now all discipline seems to be more pain than pleasure at the time, yet later it will produce a transformation of character, bringing a harvest of righteousness and peace to those who yield to it." (Hebrews 12:3-11 TPT)*

The Huios of God realizes that submission is an attitude, not just an action. In other words, in the previous stages of spiritual maturity, I'm submitting because you tell me to, but as a Huios of God, I'm submitting because I understand the importance of doing so, because my motivation is to be more like Jesus. Therefore, I submit to godly authority.

> *"But he continues to pour out more and more grace upon us. For it says, God resists you when you are proud but continually pours out grace when you are humble." (James 4:6 TPT)*

The Huios of God, because of their level of maturity and authority, has to be careful that pride doesn't come and take root in their life. This happens because they've strayed away from the presence of the Father and believe that they don't need anyone to advise them, that they can do it by themselves. That's a dangerous place to be.

> *"Your plans will fall apart right in front of you if you fail to get good advice. But if you first seek out multiple counselors, you'll watch your plans succeed."* (Proverbs 15:22 TPT)

If they remain humble, this Huios of God is the son or daughter who may be sent as the full, complete representation of the Father. They may also be called and commissioned to operate in the Five-Fold Ministry, because they can be trusted to build up the Body of Christ and can be found encouraging the unity of the Spirit.

MUSING: THOUGHTS TO PROVOKE

"There are some citrus trees that have both full ripe fruit on them and blossoms at the same time. It is like that with us. In some areas we may be mature and developed and in other areas just a little bud. It is a lifelong thing. I will always be producing a crop and promising a crop at the same time." – Neva Coyle

QUESTIONS TO PONDER:

Which stage of development are you in? Are you willing to move on to the next stage of development, or are you content to stay the same?

CHAPTER 6:
OUR HELP COMES FROM THE LORD – THE FIVE GRACES

Are we our own worst enemy?

After reviewing the stages of spiritual maturation from the previous chapters, we must effectively determine which stage of spiritual growth and development we are in. We don't want to become our own worst enemy, so God has sent us spiritual help to successfully move us from one stage to the next. As a result, we won't become stagnant or be caught with arrested development.

When Jesus ascended into heaven after His resurrection, He told the disciples that He wasn't leaving them comfortless. Their concern was how they were going to make it if they didn't have Jesus in the flesh to teach them and to oversee them as they performed miracles, as they preached the Word, to help them stay out of trouble. As always, Jesus had an answer for them.

When Jesus said that He came that we might have life and have it more abundantly, He left this physical realm and gave us the responsibility and the resources to G.R.O.W.! In other words, Get Rid Of Weeds! Some of us think that after we come to Christ, we are in this race called life all by ourselves and have to rely only on our own intellect to help us through. If I try to do that, then instead of helping myself, I may only be hurting myself.

But Jesus, through His infinite love and grace, has sent help through five graces: The Holy Spirit, The Word of God, The Five-Fold Ministry, Mentors/Disciplers, and His Grace. So, let's use what's been given us so we can mature, thrive, and reproduce. Let's use them so we can grow and be fruitful, multiply, replenish, subdue, and take dominion as God originally intended for mankind in Genesis 1:28. We have no excuses not to grow and mature. I have found that for various reasons, many Christians do not readily use the resources and spiritual weapons that God has made available to us as Believers. Some don't know how to use them, some don't know they're available for every Believer to use, and some may not even know what they are. It is necessary to use all five to reap the benefits of authentic spiritual growth.

I'm going to use the analogy of the hand and fingers to describe the help that God gives Believers to spiritually grow. The number five in scripture refers to grace, and God sent the Five Helps or Graces in order for us to grow, flow, and go in God!

The Believer is represented by the hand itself, and from the hand comes the help that we need. Below is a short summary of how these Helps interact with the Believer and with each other.

The **thumb** is the only finger that can touch the other fingers, and it represents the **Holy Spirit**, which is the only one that touches and intimately works alongside the other Graces, helping them grip the life of the Believer and assist them in functioning. It is there to keep the Believer rooted and grounded as they mature. We need the Holy Spirit in order to grip and hold on to the presence of God that is constant in our lives. It doesn't matter what we are doing or saying, the Holy Spirit keeps us woke so we don't miss anything that He would say to guide and assist us in our spiritual maturation.

The **Five-Fold ministry** gifts are characterized by the **pointer** finger. They are responsible for pointing us to our purpose and keeping us on our God-given assignment. The Five-Fold ministry gifts lead a Believer into the knowledge and relationship with the Father and into their purpose, by training and preparing them for Kingdom service.

The **Word of God** is represented by the **middle** finger, the one that reaches further out than the others. God's Word is a lamp unto my feet and a light unto my path. The Word of God lights the way to growth and maturity.

The **Grace of God** is illustrated by the **ring** finger. Because of the grace of God, we are in a covenantal relationship with the Father. Because we are saved by His grace, we will always be connected and hardwired to God through His grace.

I use the **little pinky** finger to describe the relationship of the Believer to the **progenitors**: mentors, spiritual parents, and those that disciple the growing Believer. The progenitor brings strength and balance to the Believer in Christ. They help with the equipping and maturity of the Believer.

Along with the analogy of the hand and fingers to describe how the five Graces support us in our spiritual growth, we're going to use elements of the chiropractic five signs of life philosophy as well. As we navigate through this section, you will begin to see the different ways God gives us the assistance and support to become that fully grown and mature (teleios) Believer in Jesus Christ.

My second oldest daughter is a chiropractor. There were times when I would ask her why she chose the chiropractic field as part of her life's work. She related to me that part of her reason for becoming a chiropractor is their philosophy. She explained that chiropractors believe that God created the body to be a well-organized, self-healing, self-regulating system. She further stated that the nervous system controls every bodily function, and if there is interference in your nervous system, it can prevent the healthy function of any of the other systems in your body. This is where dis-ease can occur in our body. The chiropractor removes the interference by way of the chiropractic adjustment, which allows us to heal and function the way God created our bodies to do.

So, how does the chiropractic philosophy relate to a Believer's authentic spiritual growth? By using our fleshly desires, the devil wants to have the preeminence in our lives and overtake us to the point that we are unable to truly know God as our Father and His love and purpose for us. The devil's purpose is to interfere with what God wants to do with our lives, thereby causing dis-ease in our souls. But the purpose of these five Graces is to aid in the spiritual adjustments that we need to remove the spiritual interferences that stand in the way of our growth and maturity, so that we are able to heal and function as God created us. Now, it is no longer the devil and our interfering flesh that has the preeminence, but we have embraced the Christ in us. Now, neither the devil, nor temptation, nor the world system can have any dominion over us.

The philosophy of chiropractic care identifies five signs of life that lets you know that something is alive and functioning: **Assimilation, Excretion, Adaptability, Growth,** and **Reproduction**. Let's look at these five areas and begin to process how they relate to our authentic spiritual growth and the help God has given us! As we go through each of the five Graces, I'm also going to use these five signs of life to describe the importance of spiritual maturation.

Assimilation is the ability of your body to absorb certain foods that will aid in your growth.

Excretion is its ability to eliminate the waste and toxins that the cells in your body produce.

Adaptability is how your body responds to all the forces, stress, and trouble that come against it.

Growth is characterized by the body's specific maturation process that allows it to develop in both the amount and direction of growth.

Reproduction is a vital sign of life because it replaces the damaged and dead tissues and cells with brand new ones.

In the following sections in this chapter, I will describe and connect the five chiropractic signs of life with the five Helps that God has given us to assist us through our spiritual maturation.

THE HOLY SPIRIT

"The Thumb"
Partnership

> *"As you yield freely and fully to the dynamic life and power of the Holy Spirit, you will abandon the cravings of your self-life. For your self-life craves the things that offend the Holy Spirit and hinder him from living free within you! And the Holy Spirit's intense cravings hinder your old self-life from dominating you! So then, the two incompatible and conflicting forces within you are your self-life of the flesh and the new creation life of the Spirit." (Galatians 5:16-17 TPT)*

When I received the Holy Spirit as a young girl, with the evidence of speaking in tongues, it opened a whole new world and experience for me. It felt like I had come alive; it felt like a refreshing and cleansing inside of me. As I was taught the scriptures on this phenomenon, I realized that the Holy Spirit was a powerful resource that would aid in building me spiritually. In fact, until I was taught, I was unaware of the great help in my spiritual journey that I would receive by having the Holy Spirit. My pastors at the time were great advocates of making sure that those who came to their church would experience receiving the Holy Spirit with the evidence of speaking in tongues, as well as walking in the activation of the other eight manifestations spoken of in 1 Corinthians 12, because they understood the importance and magnitude of what that all meant in the life of the Believer. They knew what it meant for a believer not only to walk in spiritual authority and power but to have that help they need to grow in His grace and in the knowledge of our Lord and Saviour Jesus Christ.

The purpose of receiving the Holy Spirit was not just to heal the sick, raise the dead, and cast out devils. Don't get me wrong, these are very necessary activations, but that is not all the Holy Spirit was sent to do. In this section, we will explore how the Holy Spirit is necessary in the Believer's journey to authentic spiritual growth and maturity.

The very best thing that happened in my life was accepting Jesus as my Lord and Saviour and receiving the Holy Spirit. The joy and assurance of having the Holy Spirit in my life has allowed me so many great benefits and deterred me from so many mishaps and hardships.

Let's go back to the origin of this phenomenon. When Jesus walked the earth working to complete His assignment, He performed many signs, miracles, and wonders in the lives of those He came in contact with. But there came a time when He was nearing the end of His particular assignment on the earth. Of course, as Jesus really began to zero in on the fact that His assignment of giving His life as a ransom for many was coming up for completion and that He would not be with them much longer, he made more and more references to the fact that He would be leaving. When Jesus made statements about His leaving and going to prepare a place for them, the 12 disciples, His inner circle, were heartbroken. They had so many questions concerning His departure and how they would figure into this. This man Jesus, whom they had grown to know and love, was leaving them. They thought that Jesus was there to overthrow the government of that day and set up His Kingdom, and that they were going to rule with Him. That's why the sons of Zebedee and their mother asked Jesus if they could sit on His right and left sides when He set up His Kingdom.

Jesus' disciples had so many great and fascinating experiences with Him. They watched Jesus perform so many miracles and confront the Sadducees and Pharisees, the religious hypocrites during that time, with such boldness and confidence. They listened and watched as He taught the multitudes with parables about the Kingdom of God. As Jesus taught, the disciples observed the people's response to Jesus, which was like none they'd ever seen. They saw that the people couldn't get enough of Jesus and His teachings. The 12 disciples were His inner circle, and Jesus even gave them authority and sent them on spiritual assignments to preach the Word of God and perform miracles just as He did. As His inner circle, they were privy to the spiritual meanings of the parables Jesus told to the multitudes, and they basked in the attention they were receiving from being with Jesus.

The culture during that time was distinctly patriarchal, so a woman's place was in the background, more like property than like a helpmate according to God's original intent spoken of in Genesis 1 and 2. Jesus showed His disciples, through many examples in the Gospels, of women being put into their proper position according to God's original plan when He created male and female. Jesus showed compassion when the woman was brought to Him after she was accused of adultery. Women were always encouraged by Jesus, not condemned or looked down upon. He healed them, He spoke to them in public, and He allowed them to travel with him. Jesus gave women the proper respect, dignity, and authority that was due them.

What a Man, what a Man, What a Mighty Great Man! And He was going to leave the disciples all alone? That couldn't be! Jesus told His disciples that they were not going to be alone, but that He was going to send a Comforter, He was going to send a Teacher, He was going to send Power. He was sending the Holy Spirit to dwell within!

> *"If you love me, obey my commandments. And I will ask the Father, and he will give you another Advocate, who will never leave you. He is the Holy Spirit, who leads into all truth. The world cannot receive him, because it isn't looking for him and doesn't recognize him. But you know him, because he lives with you now and later will be in you." (John 14:15-17 NLT)*

> *"There is so much more I would like to say to you, but it's more than you can grasp at this moment. But when the truth-giving Spirit comes, he will unveil the reality of every truth within you. He won't speak his own message, but only what he hears from the Father, and he will reveal prophetically to you what is to come. He will glorify me on the earth, for he will receive from me what is mine and reveal it to you. Everything that belongs to the Father belongs to me—that's why I say that the Divine Encourager will receive what is mine and reveal it to you." (John 16:12-15 TPT)*

He was sending mighty Help from on High! In fact, after His resurrection, Jesus gave them a precursor of what that would look like:

> *"Then, taking a deep breath, he blew on them and said, 'Receive the Holy Spirit.'" (John 20:22 TPT)*

Jesus gave an indication in John 7:38-39 that the Holy Spirit would flow from the heart like rivers of living water. "Rheo" is the Greek word for "flow" in verse 38 pictures a rushing stream that is so full that it overflows the banks of the water. Jesus was saying that the Holy Spirit that is coming is going to be overflowing and continuously active in the life of the Believer.

Acts 2 chronicles the outpouring of the Holy Spirit by Jesus as He promised to the disciples in Acts 1:8.

> *"But I promise you this—the Holy Spirit will come upon you and you will be filled with power. And you will be my messengers to Jerusalem, throughout Judea, the distant provinces—even to the remotest places on earth!" (Acts 1:8 TPT)*

Jesus said they would be filled with Power from on High when the Holy Spirit comes upon them. This power spoken of in Acts 1:8 is from the Greek word "dunamis," which is where we get our word dynamite from. This spiritual dynamite power is regenerative power. It's power that doesn't stop, nor does it run out. It continues and continues. In the King James version of Acts 1:8, Jesus says, "ye shall receive power." Receive is from the Greek word "lambano," which means it is an active reception, not a passive reception. In other words, it means that when I receive power, I'm going to do something with it. It will not lie dormant in me! It will be activated in my life and throughout my life.

In Ephesians 1:13, Paul assures us by stating that we have been sealed with the Holy Spirit that was promised to us. The Holy Spirit is here to stay.

> *"In Him, you also, after listening to the message of truth, the gospel of your salvation—having also believed, you were sealed in Him with the Holy Spirit of promise." (NASB)*

When I accepted Jesus Christ, I received power from on High. I received the Holy Spirit that abides in me. It's a permanent habitation. The Holy Spirit is not an occasional visitor that comes and goes. He is not an emotional feeling that isn't there if I don't feel Him. But we can minimize the Holy Spirit's influence when we allow other influences, like our own flesh and the devil, to interfere with the workings of the Holy Spirit. The Holy Spirit is here to stay with me in my heart, ready, willing, and able to do what He was sent to do in my life to help me fulfill purpose. That means I have to build a relationship with Him by spending time with Him.

Not only was I given eternal life, redemption in Jesus' Blood, and sonship rights when I accepted Jesus Christ, but I was also given a Helper, a Teacher, a Trainer, a Counselor, an Encourager, a Guide, a Deliverer, a Friend, an Advocate through the workings of the gift of the Holy Spirit. The Holy Spirit of God abides in us with wisdom, knowledge and power. The Holy Spirit is willing and able to connect and partner with us as He comes alongside us and helps us!

How do we know that we have the Holy Spirit? It's through the outward workings: the nine active demonstrations or expressions of the Holy Spirit spoken of in 1 Corinthians 12:1-11. We have for our use Word of Wisdom, Word of Knowledge, Faith, Healings, Miracles, Prophecy, Discerning of Spirits, Tongues, and Interpretation of Tongues. They are there for us to use if we take the time to learn to operate in them.

I previously mentioned the five signs of life that are part of the chiropractic philosophy and how they parallel the help that God has given us to have authentic spiritual growth and maturation.

Remember, I said **Assimilation** is what the body takes in and absorbs to aid in growth. Well, when you accept Jesus Christ as Lord and Saviour, you also take in or receive the Holy Spirit. The Holy Spirit aids in our spiritual maturation by bringing to our attention the areas of our life that we need to transform. Not only that, when we assimilate, we are also taking in or absorbing by listening to the Holy Spirit. Communication by prayer is a very important factor.

> *"Don't be pulled in different directions or worried about a thing. Be saturated in prayer throughout each day, offering your faith-filled requests before God with overflowing gratitude. Tell him every detail of your life." (Philippians 4:6 TPT)*

That then brings us to **Excretion,** which allows wastes and toxins to be removed from us. The Holy Spirit brings to our attention the areas in our lives that hinder us from walking in our purpose, fulfilling our assignment, and walking in our destiny. The Holy Spirit lets us know that those areas—like unforgiveness, pride, and the works of the flesh spoken of in Galatians 5:19-21—need to be excreted and eliminated from our mind, will, emotions, and heart. The Holy Spirit helps us recognize those works of the flesh that need to be eliminated from our lives because they hinder our spiritual growth and development. They limit the plan and purposes God has for our lives. They are toxins, and we know toxins can cause disease and harm to the mind, soul, and heart. If we participate in these works of the flesh, our mindset, attitude, and actions come across to others as toxic and, as a result, become self-defeating and self-destructive.

> *"The cravings of the self-life are obvious: Sexual immorality, lustful thoughts, pornography, chasing after things instead of God manipulating others, hatred of those who get in your way, senseless arguments, resentment when others are favored, temper tantrums, angry quarrels, only thinking of yourself, being in love with your own opinions, being envious of the blessings of others, murder, uncontrolled addictions, wild parties, and all other similar behavior. Haven't I already warned you that those who use their 'freedom' for these things will not inherit the kingdom realm of God!" (Galatians 5:19-21 TPT)*

Here's an example of not crucifying the old fleshly and demonic practices. In my years of ministry, I've come across Believers who were knee-deep in the occult before they came to Christ, and when they came to Christ and were filled with the Holy Spirit, instead of getting rid of the occultic practices, they tried to immerse them into Christianity. It's almost like, just in case the Holy Spirit can't do it, they'll rely on the occultic practice. Saints, we cannot mix the pure Holy Spirit with the impure occult if we want to have authentic spiritual growth. When we have mixture, it always leads to self-destruction.

> *"You can't hold the holy cup of the Lord in one hand and the cup of demons in the other. You can't share in the Lord's table while picking off the altar of demons."*
> *(1 Corinthians 10:21 Voice)*

The Holy Spirit brings these things to our attention, but it's up to us to listen and cooperate with the Holy Spirit as He tells us how to eliminate the works of the flesh so we can live with a transformed, renewed mind and our attitude and actions will mirror those of our Lord Jesus Christ. That's the state we want to live in!

> *"You must have the same attitude that Christ Jesus had."*
> *(Philippians 2:5 NLT)*

Adaptability is the next area that determines the signs of life for a Believer and how the Holy Spirit helps us. Adaptability is how our body responds to all the stress and trouble that comes against us. The Holy Spirit has been given to us to help us combat and correctly respond to the stress and troubles that plague us as we go through what we call life!

I remember when my family and I were under tremendous stress because sickness and disease had hit hard and heavy. If we had not partnered with and relied on the Holy Spirit to rescue us, we would have buckled under the stress and pressure, given up, and given in to it. As we spent time speaking to Him and listening to Him, the Holy Spirit began to speak and pour out words of encouragement to us to calm us down. The Holy Spirit gave us Word of Knowledge and Word of Wisdom so we would make the right decisions. Through the workings of the Holy Spirit, we were able to discern what medical care was needed and what we needed to discard. As a result, we came out victorious! The Holy Spirit helps in our weakness.

We have to make sure that we are communicating with the Holy Spirit at all times and allowing Him to do what He is sent to do for us and through us! The Holy Spirit gives us access to our Father God. Sometimes we don't know what to say or how to pray in our own native language, but when we begin to speak in tongues, the heavenly language that was given to us on the Day of Pentecost, the Holy Spirit communicates with God our Father and lets Him know our needs. The Holy Spirit knows far better than us what we need. Our Father God sends help in the time of that need!

> *"And in a similar way, the Holy Spirit takes hold of us in our human frailty to empower us in our weakness. For example, at times we don't even know how to pray, or know the best things to ask for. But the Holy Spirit rises up within us to super-intercede on our behalf, pleading to God with emotional sighs too deep for words." Romans 8:26 TPT*

The next sign of life for the Believer is **Growth**, which is part of the maturation process. The Holy Spirit definitely assists us in helping us grow and mature. We have the promise that the Holy Spirit will oversee our growth and bring us to maturity. I may not see or know what I need to do to bring myself to maturity, but I don't have to do it alone; the Holy Spirit knows what to do. So, I partner with Him, and if I'm wise, He becomes the senior partner. He's the indwelling Helper.

> *"He who began a good work in you will carry it on to completion until the day of Christ Jesus."*
> *(Philippians 1:6 NIV)*

> *"I pray with great faith for you, because I'm fully convinced that the One who began this glorious work in you will faithfully continue the process of maturing you and will put his finishing touches to it until the unveiling of our Lord Jesus Christ!" (Philippians 1:6 TPT)*

The last of the five signs of life is **Reproduction**. Reproduction replaces the old with the new. The Holy Spirit aids in that process by showing us how to walk in newness of life and in the resurrecting power of Jesus Christ. As we are walking in the resurrecting power of Jesus Christ, we have an opportunity to reproduce that power by example.

> *"This is why the Scriptures say: Things never discovered or heard of before, things beyond our ability to imagine—these are the many things God has in store for all his lovers. But God now unveils these profound realities to us by the Spirit. Yes, he has revealed to us his inmost heart and deepest mysteries through the Holy Spirit, who constantly explores*

all things. After all, who can really see into a person's heart and know his hidden impulses except for that person's spirit? So it is with God. His thoughts and secrets are only fully understood by his Spirit, the Spirit of God. For we did not receive the spirit of this world system but the Spirit of God, so that we might come to understand and experience all that grace has lavished upon us. And we articulate these realities with the words imparted to us by the Spirit and not with the words taught by human wisdom. We join together Spirit-revealed truths with Spirit-revealed words."
(1 Corinthians 2:9-13 TPT)

> **MUSING: THOUGHTS TO PROVOKE**
>
> "Let yourselves be led by the Holy Spirit, with freedom and, please, do not cage the Holy Spirit." – Pope Francis
>
> **QUESTIONS TO PONDER:**
>
> How am I allowing the Holy Spirit to be that Helper, Teacher, Encourager that helps bring me to authentic growth and maturity?

THE HOLY BIBLE

"Middle Finger"
Lights the Way

"He sendeth forth his commandment upon earth; his word runneth very swiftly." (Psalm 147:15 KJV)

God's logos Word, which is His written Word and what we call the Bible, tells of His will and His ways! If we want to grow in

Have we found the many hidden treasures in Christ?

His grace and in the knowledge of our Lord and Saviour Jesus Christ, we must spend time in His Word, because it reveals so much of who God is, His love, and His plan of redemption for mankind! His Word is a treasury of promises and blessings that are not hidden from those who consistently read His Word. The Word of God not only reveals to us the importance of maturity but also explains to us what we need to do to mature.

The Word of God not only tells us so much about the power and the authority of the Blood of Jesus, it expresses our rights as Kingdom citizens and speaks about God's promises. It reveals to us who we are and who we belong to. The Word tells us that we are fearfully and wonderfully made. Scriptures reveal Jesus Christ our Messiah in each book of the Bible, from Genesis to Revelation. The Word of God makes clear the will of God, the way of God, and the purposes of God.

God's Word is so powerful that He puts it above His name! God backs His Word by the power and greatness of His name, which shows us that He is true to His Word.

> *"I bow down before your divine presence and bring you my deepest worship as I experience your tender love and your living truth. For the promises of your word and the fame of your name have been magnified above all else!" (Psalm 138:2 TPT)*

There is so much richness in God's Word. It gives us instruction for marriage, life, and love. God's Word gives us encouragement, it convicts us to do right, and it's full of the description of God's power that is available to us as Believers. The Word of God is for our instruction, correction, protection, and direction!

> *"All scripture is given by inspiration of God, and is profitable for doctrine, for reproof, for correction, for instruction in righteousness: That the man of God may be perfect, thoroughly furnished unto all good works."*
> *(2 Timothy 3:16-17 KJV)*

The Word of God comes straight from God, from His very breath. Just as God breathed into Adam the breath of life and he became a living soul, so has He breathed out His Word so that it becomes life to all who read and believe it. The Word of God is beneficial to instruct us, to convict us, to correct us, and to teach us about God's righteousness so that we don't stray and continue the practice of sin. We are washed by the water of the Word that we might be a glorious church, holy, without spot or wrinkle. God's Word is not just words on a page – The Word of God is alive and vibrant, and it works!

> *"For we have the living Word of God, which is full of energy, and it pierces more sharply than a two-edged sword. It will even penetrate to the very core of our being where soul and spirit, bone and marrow meet! It interprets and reveals the true thoughts and secret motives of our hearts."* (Hebrews 4:12 TPT)

The Word of God can discern our true thoughts and the very intentions and secret motives of our hearts. Those are some powerful words! In other words, as we read the Word of God, it reveals to us the deep things in our hearts and challenges us to make the necessary changes so that our hearts will be more like the heart of God.

How does the Word of God provide **Assimilation** as we grow spiritually? When we assimilate, we are absorbing what we need in order to grow. The Word of God provides that, because as we read and absorb it, it gives us the necessary spiritual nutrients for our mind, will, and emotions, as well as our heart, to authentically grow. For example, when I read in the Bible that we are to love one another, and that love is of God and everyone that loves is born of God, and that God is love, according to 1 John 4:7-8, then I begin to apply His Word and allow love to land and abide in me. I absorb love and become a carrier of it.

> *"Let the word of Christ live in you richly, flooding you with all wisdom. Apply the Scriptures as you teach and instruct one another with the Psalms, and with festive praises, and with prophetic songs given to you spontaneously by the Spirit, so sing to God with all your hearts!" (Colossians 3:16 TPT)*

As we **Assimilate** by reading and absorbing the truth of God's Word, it will lead us to repentance, which allows us to eliminate the areas in our hearts and minds that are contrary to the Word of God and that our sinful nature so craves and wants. As we read His Word, if there is any wickedness in us – and I'm sure there is – we will let go of it by eliminating everything that hinders our spiritual walk towards authentic spiritual growth, anything that can get in the way of our relationship with our Father God. For example, as

I read God's Word in Galatians 5:19-21 about the works of our sinful nature, I begin to **Eliminate** those toxic areas in my life that limit me from fulfilling God's plan for my life. When I read about the importance of forgiveness, I have to examine myself, and if I harbor unforgiveness, it benefits my whole body, will, and emotions to eliminate unforgiveness in me so that I can live a holy and peaceful life. If I'm a doer of the Word, then I must do what the Word says!

> *"Make allowance for each other's faults, and forgive anyone who offends you. Remember, the Lord forgave you, so you must forgive others." (Colossians 3:13 NLT)*

Recently, my husband and I decided to clean out our garage and basement. Well, as we looked around those two areas, we realized we had a lot of junk that we needed to discard. In fact, it was a substantial amount of junk that we had held on to for years. So, we decided we needed a dumpster. When they delivered it, I didn't think we needed all that space for the amount of junk we had accumulated. Boy, was I wrong! As our sons began to put things inside the dumpster, I realized that, in fact, the dumpster might not be big enough for all that we had collected and didn't need. It can be the same as we read the Word of God and apply it to the "junk" within ourselves. We don't think that we have to do much cleaning or eliminating out of our lives until we honestly, genuinely, and sincerely look at ourselves as we ingest the Word of God and allow it to be a cleansing and healing agent.

The Word of God needs to richly dwell in us. God designed it to come alive in us and through us. His Word is called the Living

Word, and the only way that can happen is if we study and accept His Word so that it begins to dwell in our hearts. In other words, we have to read His Word, speak His Word, pray His Word, and do what His Word says. God's Word is valuable and invaluable!

> *"Don't just listen to the Word of Truth and not respond to it, for that is the essence of self-deception. So always let his Word become like poetry written and fulfilled by your life!"* (James 1:22 TPT

> *"Your word I have treasured and stored in my heart, That I may not sin against You." (Psalm 119:11 Amplified Bible)*

My **Adaptability** to God's Word allows me to face situations and circumstances that are way past my human understanding, and to do so without being overwhelmed, hopeless, stressed, depressed, and in a mess. With His Word, I live above all circumstances, not below them. Because I'm reading and comprehending His Word, I begin to believe and do what the Word says to do.

I used this example earlier when referring to the Holy Spirit's help. When my family was faced with sickness and disease that hit us hard and heavy, not only was the Holy Spirit with us, the Word of God was in us! When we began to read and listen to the Word of God, especially on the subject of healing and His provision, the Word of God began to uplift, encourage, enlighten, and rejuvenate us, and it started the process of healing and wholeness. I always say, give God something to work with. There is so much power in His Word!

There is so much in Scripture that speaks about **Growth** and the spiritual maturation of a Believer. The Word speaks specifically of how important it is for us as Believers to become mature in Him so that we can fulfill the purpose and the assignment He has given us. This will allow us, with the help of the Holy Spirit, to let the fruit of the spirit spoken of in Galatians 5:22-23 be an outward showing of the crucified life and the resurrected life!

> *"My old identity has been co-crucified with Messiah and no longer lives; for the nails of his cross crucified me with him. And now the essence of this new life is no longer mine, for the Anointed One lives his life through me—we live in union as one! My new life is empowered by the faith of the Son of God who loves me so much that he gave himself for me, and dispenses his life into mine!" (Galatians 2:20 TPT)*

Jesus was all about **Reproduction**, and he speaks of it expressly in the Word of God when He commands all of His followers to make disciples. It's not enough that we as Believers just stay concerned about "me, myself, and I"; in our maturity, it is important to remain disciples of Christ and make disciples of Christ. Jesus was not talking about individual churches growing in numbers but about us giving of ourselves into the lives of others.

> *"Now go in my authority and make disciples of all nations, baptizing them in the name of the Father, the Son, and the Holy Spirit." (Matthew 28:19 TPT)*

So, let us use His Word to direct us, because as we read and follow His Words, we shall have great success as we continue to grow and mature in Christ!

MUSING: THOUGHTS TO PROVOKE

"So often we are in danger of abusing the Scriptures... We use them as mere phrases in that manner, or lightheartedly we sing our hymns, and we feel better for the time being. But the question is, How do we stand up to temptations when we are in the street outside, and what are we like at home? When you turn Scripture into a drug, into something which gives you a temporary relief without your knowing why or how, the effect does not last. It gives a temporary feeling of exhilaration, but fails you when you are in the struggle and in the heat of the battle." – Martyn Lloyd-Jones

QUESTIONS TO PONDER:

How is the Word of God specifically helping you to Assimilate, Excrete, Adapt, Grow, and Reproduce?

THE FIVE-FOLD MINISTRY

"Pointer Finger"
Pointing the way to purpose, maturity, and unity

"So Christ himself gave the apostles, the prophets, the evangelists, the pastors and teachers, to equip his people for works of service, so that the body of Christ may be built up until we all reach unity in the faith and in the knowledge of the Son of God and become mature, attaining to the whole measure of the fullness of Christ." (Ephesians 4:11-13 NIV)

OUR HELP COMES FROM THE LORD – THE FIVE GRACES

During a basketball game, each team has five members on the court at any given moment to play the game. Their goal is to win the game. They don't all have the same position; each player on the team has a particular job, a particular function, and each one has a role to play that's vital to the team's strategy for winning. Similarly, the hand has five fingers, and each finger has a different role in order for the hand to function properly and effectively.

The term "Five-Fold ministry" comes from Ephesians 4:11-13, where it mentions that Jesus gave five ministry roles to disciple, equip, and help mature the Body of Christ so they can be fruitful. Jesus gave the Body of Christ Apostles, Prophets, Evangelists, Pastors, and Teachers to help grow up the Saints of God. These roles are also called the Ascension gifts, because Jesus gave them out after He ascended into heaven. These gifts were given to bring the Body of Christ to the fullness and completion of the Christ in us.

Those who function in these roles must be at a level of maturity themselves to be unselfish, powerful men and women of God, love God's people, and be impactful in their lives by moving them to maturity so God's people can do the work of the ministry, the work of service in the Kingdom of God.

"Care for the flock that God has entrusted to you. Watch over it willingly, not grudgingly—not for what you will

> get out of it, but because you are eager to serve God."
> 1 Peter 5:2 NLT

It is important for people of God to follow godly men and women who are part of the Five-Fold ministry gifts. Because God has given them the responsibility like parents to equip, empower, and raise the people of God in the area of maturity, they have care over you, so it is important to listen, learn, and do. Don't have the rebellious attitude that nobody can tell you what to do. We live in an age of rebellion and disrespect for authority. I always say that children are a barometer of what's going in our culture and time, and even the children are showing such disrespect for their parents, teachers, and other authority figures.

> "Obey your spiritual leaders and recognize their authority, for they keep watch over your soul without resting since they will have to give an account to God for their work. So it will benefit you when you make their work a pleasure and not a heavy burden."
> (Hebrews 13:17 TPT)

The Five-Fold ministry is an extension of Christ Himself. He was our Apostle in Hebrews 3:1; our Prophet in Luke 24:19; our Evangelist in Matthew 9:35; our Pastor/Shepherd in 1 Peter 5:2-4; and our Teacher in John 3:2.

It would be wonderful if every church had the Five-Fold ministry gifts in its operation. The presence of these gifts in a church exposes the members to a well-rounded ministry that connects the areas of ministry to the Saints of God as Jesus intended when He released the Five-Fold after His ascension. Jesus wants the Saints to have the influence and benefit of each of the Five-Fold so that they will have the opportunity to thrive and flourish as they grow in Him.

The Apostle Paul stated in Colossians 1:28-29 that his purpose was to preach, instruct, rebuke, and proclaim the Word of God to the Body of Christ. Many Apostles, Prophets, Evangelists, Pastors, and Teachers over the world labor tirelessly, lovingly, and endlessly with the people of God to see them come to a full and complete maturity in Christ. You may never know their names, nor do they have notoriety. They may not even be named on social media, and they don't even care to be. Instead, their sole focus, concern, and purpose is that the Believer will no longer allow the flesh nor the world to have the preeminence in their lives, but as they grow, mature, and put on the mind of Christ more and more each day, they will experience the fullness of Christ in them, the hope of Glory.

> *"We proclaim Him, warning and instructing everyone in all wisdom [that is, with comprehensive insight into the word and purposes of God], so that we may present every person complete in Christ [mature, fully trained, and perfect in Him—the Anointed]. For this I labor [often to the point of exhaustion], striving with His power and energy, which so greatly works within me."* (Colossians 1:28-29 Amplified Bible)

I just have to say a little bit about my husband James, who has been in ministry since 1977. James, who is an Apostle, is a wonderful example of a Five-Fold ministry man of God. He was 27 years old when he was ordained as a minister and commissioned to go to Cincinnati, Ohio, to pastor a young church. Of course, as his wife, I came along. We were pregnant with our first child, and we didn't know much about pastoring, but we were well equipped as leaders by our Pastors. His love and concern for people is outstanding, as well as his passion for God. I've watched him labor and pray so intensely, earnestly, and tirelessly over the lives of others until he either felt a breakthrough or the Holy Spirit said "that's it." There were plenty of times he became discouraged, but he never gave up and never gave in, because he listens to the inward voice of the Holy Spirit, he's empowered by the grace of God, he's mentored by various people, he stays in the Word of God, and he listens to other Five-Fold ministries so that he can continue to spiritually grow.

Apostle James preaches, instructs, rebukes, and proclaims the Word of God, and he challenges the Body of Christ to walk and function in the call of God. Sometimes his ways in doing this were – and still can be – unorthodox, and the way he expounds on the Word of God is both humorous and challenging. One of the things I love and respect about him is that his heart is after God's heart, and that is to see the people of God, those he has care over, become the manifested sons and daughters of God who are walking in the wholeness and completeness of Christ, passionately living in God's purpose. I love me some James Blue!!

How does the Five-Fold ministry allow us to **Assimilate**, **Excrete**, **Grow**, **Adapt**, and **Reproduce** as it pertains to the signs of life in the Believer? In Assimilation, the Pastor guards, feeds, and cares for the people of God to make sure they are getting the proper spiritual nourishment that will aid in the Believer's spiritual maturation and growth.

Remember, **Assimilation** is what the body takes in and absorbs to aid in growth. I believe since the Pastor guards, their responsibility and commitment is to make sure the Body of Christ is properly trained and feeding on the Word of God so they can authentically grow in His grace.

In the area of **Excretion**, the Prophet guides. The Prophet is the eyes and ears of the Body of Christ, and in this area, they make sure that the people of God don't allow anything to interfere with the presence of God in their lives. They bring the voice of the Lord to help lead and point us to righteousness!

For **Adaptability**, we'll use the Evangelist as an example. As the gatherer, the Evangelist brings to the attention of the people of God not only the need for salvation but the need to look to Jesus as the solution to problems. The Evangelist keeps our focus on Jesus, not on our problems.

The Teacher is a great example of **Growth** because the Teacher is a grounder; they illuminate and clarify the truth of God's Word. By doing this, the Teacher helps construct in the life of the Believer a strong foundation and deep roots in the things of God, producing the capacity to grow up authentically in Christ.

For **Reproduction**, the Apostle is a wonderful example. Not only does the Apostle govern, but their heart is the advancement of the Kingdom of God. As a result, the Apostle sends the mature Believer in Jesus Christ out of the four walls of the church into the world to make disciples, to reproduce, and to advance the Kingdom of God in the earth.

MUSING: THOUGHTS TO PROVOKE

"We have to know that one of the great marks of spiritual maturity is being able to take admonition and rebuke! This matter of being able to admit faults and seek to correct them is a mark of maturity." – Max Forsythe

QUESTIONS TO PONDER:

How is each one of the Five-Fold Ministries supporting you in your authentic spiritual growth and maturity?

PROGENITORS

"Pinky Finger"
Bringing balance

"We have a lot of believers in churches. Big deal! The devil believes, but he is not a disciple. We need disciples!"
– Unknown or Paraphrased

"We have a lot of leaders in churches. Big deal! The devil has leaders too, but they lead others to death and destruction. We need godly leaders that lead others to Christ's abundant life and God's purpose!" – Grace Blue

There are Believers who sit in the church pews and never realize their purpose, nor the plan of God for their lives. Even if they know God has a calling or plan for their life, they do not know how to go about fulfilling God's purpose. They need someone to lead and direct them.

> *"So search your hearts every day, my brothers and sisters, and make sure that none of you has evil or unbelief hiding within you. For it will lead you astray, and make you unresponsive to the living God. This is the time to encourage each other to never be stubborn or hardened by sin's deceitfulness." (Hebrews 3:12-13 TPT)*

> *"Iron sharpens iron, and one man sharpens another." (Proverbs 27:17 ESV)*

Progenitor is a term used to describe "a person that first indicates a direction, originates something, or serves as a model; predecessor; or a precursor." For my intents and purposes, the spiritual Progenitors in the Body of Christ are composed of Mentors, those who disciple Believers, and Spiritual Parents. They are vital to the spiritual maturation of the Believer. They themselves are overcomers and are mature enough to reproduce godly individuals who are overcomers also. The Progenitor is a life-long learner and a person of godly character and integrity. The Progenitor comes alongside a growing Believer and can correct, protect, and direct them in their spiritual growth and development.

For clarity's sake, many people view a mentor as one who spends most of their time with one person to impart knowledge and information, or as one who not only imparts knowledge but also gets more involved in a person's life and helps to correct behavior by modeling based on the goal or target set. I'm not talking about that type of mentoring as a way of leading one to authentic spiritual growth, but about a deeper level of mentoring or discipleship that Jesus mentioned in Matthew 28:19-20.

> *"Now go in my authority and make **disciples** of all nations, baptizing them in the name of the Father, the Son, and the Holy Spirit. And teach them to faithfully follow all that I have commanded you. And never forget that I am with you every day, even to the completion of this age." (TPT)*

When Jesus commanded His disciples to go and make disciples of all nations, to baptize them and teach them to observe all that He commanded them, he was not just talking about imparting basic knowledge of Him. As a true disciple, a person not only learns what the teacher teaches but also becomes like the teacher. Progenitors don't have to be one of the Five-Fold ministries spoken about earlier, but they do need to be at a level of maturity that shows they have the capacity to help lead and catapult one into the perfect will of God. It cannot be someone who is intimidated by their growing Believer because of their anointing and call.

Progenitors are key to the successful growth of the Believer. As a Progenitor, you're able to reproduce spiritual children of your own. To successfully impart into a growing Believer, a Progenitor should be in the Huios stage of spiritual growth and development.

I have had such a wonderful mentor and spiritual mother in my life in the likes of Bishop Patricia T. Whitelocke. As I mentioned before, she is an incredible visionary and one who loves and serves God with all of her heart. She has had a powerful impact on my life. If God hadn't allowed her to mentor and disciple me, I don't know what other path I would have followed, but I certainly know that it wouldn't have been the path God wanted me to be on. I must also say that she is not only a mentor but also part of the Five-Fold ministry gifts.

I could name so many examples of the ways that Bishop Whitelocke has impacted my life. I don't even know if she realizes the sacrificial deposits she invested in my life and the lives of others. As I stated previously, she is a visionary, emancipator, equipper, and so much more. She truly loves and cares about people. Being around Bishop Whitelocke and her ministry, I have observed many miracles, healings, and deliverances. When I was so shy and unsure of myself as a young girl, she viewed me through the lens of the Holy Spirit and saw that there was greatness in me, and she was determined to pull it out of me. For that, I'm forever grateful! She took the time and the energy to focus on me, and many others like me, because her heart was and still is after the will, the word, and the purposes of God in the lives of others.

Bishop Whitelocke provided my husband and me with so many opportunities to grow, especially with her guiding wisdom, insight, and example. She took my husband and me on our first missionary trip months after we were married. During the times she exposed us to international missions, when she was unable to travel as much, we were provided with an innate love and desire to continue with those trips abroad, even taking others. She models the walk of Christ, the love of God, and the power of the Holy Spirit. Thank you, Bishop Whitelocke, you certainly challenged me to greatness in God!

> *"My beloved friends, imitate my walk with God and follow all those who walk according to the way of life we modeled before you." (Philippians 3:17 TPT)*

Progenitors like Bishop Whitelocke help build capacity and raise your bar. They won't allow you to be comfortable in previous victories. They push you for more. They look at you through the lens of the Holy Spirit. They discern your capacity and work towards enabling you to reach and expand that capacity. They discern the purposes of God for your life and begin to challenge you to greatness. Their ultimate goal is to see Christ formed in you, as it says in Galatians 4:19. Not only do they challenge you, but they themselves are disciples of Christ. Paul said it best in 1 Corinthians 11:1.

> *"Imitate me, just as I also imitate Christ." (NKJV)*

Progenitors help in the **Assimilation** stage by showing and pointing us to those areas that will help nurture us and aid us to spiritually grow and develop. They discern the areas of a person's gift and calling and begin to point them in the direction that will aid in building capacity for maturity.

Progenitors help in the process of the **Excretion** stage by bringing to a person's attention those areas that can hinder their growth and development. It is important that the mentee and disciple listen and take heed to the one God has put in their life to help develop them and, in many ways, protect them.

In the **Adaptability** stage, the Progenitor can help the growing Believer overcome adversity, stress, and challenges by always pointing them to Jesus. They can discern; they can pray with and for the Believer. They can advise the Believer to make a decision when necessary, get some rest when needed, and pray without ceasing, and they can use other means to help them be victorious in their lives by having that "more than a conqueror" mindset. The Progenitor shows them how to adapt by using their spiritual resources, not to cave in and give up!

Progenitors help tremendously with the **Growth stage**. They are not only showing by their example, but they are challenging their mentee/disciple to continue to mature. They don't allow them to wallow in self-pity, defeatism, or self-indulgence, but continue to encourage them to advance and progress towards the higher calling in Christ Jesus.

Progenitors help the growing Believer in the **Reproduction** stage by reminding them that God birthed them onto this planet because He wanted them not only to give Him glory but also to influence others with their lives. The Progenitor's goal is to remind them that it's not all about them. Jesus said that Believers are to be light and salt. In order to be light and salt, they must invite others to taste and see that the Lord is good! Jesus' commandment before He ascended was for the disciples to make disciples. That, my friends, is reproduction!

Embrace those that God has put in your life to help you mature. Embrace the correction they give. Embrace and allow them to direct you to the greater in God. If you do, you will gain great success!

MUSING: THOUGHTS TO PROVOKE

"For many years, I pleaded with God to bring people to me who would hold me up. I believed I was too broken and weak to stand on my own. In His wisdom, He didn't answer my prayer the way I thought He should. He provided me with wise mentors who opened my eyes to this truth. I would never develop an inner strength without facing adversity head on. They provided me with the tools I needed, God provided me with His empowering grace, and it was up to me to allow my roots to grow deep. It was up to me to face adversity head on and to not retreat." – Katherine Walden

QUESTIONS TO PONDER:

Who do you have in your life that you know God has put there to aid in your spiritual maturity? What are you doing to cooperate with them?

HIS AMAZING GRACE

"Ring Finger"
Connected

"But by the grace of God I am what I am: and his grace which was bestowed upon me was not in vain; but I laboured more abundantly than they all: yet not I, but the grace of God which was with me." (1 Corinthians 15:10 KJV)

As I mentioned before, my mom had intended to give me up for adoption after I was born, but God needed for her to keep me. When she made the decision to keep me, she had to come up with a name for me. She related to me that over the loudspeaker in the hospital, they regularly called for a particular nun who was a nurse in the hospital, Sister Grace Marie. As she continued to hear that name, she decided to name me Grace Marie. For many years growing up, I did not appreciate the name Grace and sometimes wished that I had another name. God was really trying to get my attention when my classmates would call me Amazing Grace. Even with all that, I still didn't come to the realization of what my name meant. But since coming into the knowledge and understanding of God's Word, I have gained a greater awareness of the significance of the name that I believe and know God bestowed upon me. I am humbled by that name and repentant in the fact that I let years go by before I began to intentionally embrace and walk in that name, Grace. Let's delve into **Grace** and how it aids us in authentic spiritual growth and maturity.

The word Grace can be summed up in these words: the undeserved mercy, love, forgiveness, sufficiency, strength, enablement, power, gift, favor, generosity, lovingkindness, and help that we receive from the God of all Grace who has called us into His eternal glory! He has given us His Grace, which is, for us who are battling temptation, the power within us to say no to sin. There is an empowering Grace that comes with us as believers, and it is only given by God. When we take hold of His Grace and move forward, the heaviness or hardness of our circumstances is no longer overwhelming or hopeless. His Grace settles on and in our hearts, mind, and emotions to let us know that it is not by our power nor by our strength, but by His spirit that we are more than conquerors and overcomers in every situation. Grace is actually part of God's character.

Grace also defines the gift, place, and assignment that God has appointed us to. You don't feel intimidated when you walk in the gift you are given by God. His Grace allows you to do what you're called to do with confidence and enjoyment. It's like finding that sweet spot where you know no one can do what you do because His Grace is upon you to do it. Because of His Grace, your gift can bring you before great men and women! The Apostle Paul said it best:

> *"But God's amazing grace has made me who I am! And his grace to me was not fruitless. In fact, I worked harder than all the rest, yet not in my own strength but God's, for his empowering grace is poured out upon me." (1 Corinthians 15:10 TPT)*

Ephesians 2:8 says that it was by His Grace through faith that we have been saved from our sins to receive eternal life. It was not by anything that we've done to deserve it. It's God's gift to us. We can't even brag and claim that we did it on our own merits and abilities.

> *"For it was only through this wonderful grace that we believed in him. Nothing we did could ever earn this salvation, for it was the gracious gift from God that brought us to Christ! So no one will ever be able to)boast, for salvation is never a reward for good works or human striving." (Ephesians 2:8-9 TPT)*

There is an acronym that describes God's Grace: G.R.A.C.E., God's Riches At Christ's Expense. It was because of Jesus' obedience, which resulted in the sacrifice of His body for us, that we receive the undeserved Grace of God upon our lives. According to John 1:16, because of the fullness and completion of the redemptive work of Jesus Christ, we have received Grace heaped on top of Grace, spiritual blessings upon spiritual blessings. That's a beautiful thing!

> *"For out of His fullness [the superabundance of His grace and truth] we have all received grace upon grace [spiritual blessing upon spiritual blessing, favor upon favor, and gift heaped upon gift]. For the Law was given through Moses, but grace [the unearned, undeserved favor of God] and truth came through Jesus Christ." (John 1:16-17 Amplified Bible)*

As I said before, my family experienced several health crises that could have been devastating to us all. But it was God's Grace that enabled us with the strength, the power, the love, and the help to come through victoriously. It was His Grace that accompanied us through each health challenge. God's Grace wasn't only given for our salvation; it is a constant that is with us through every challenge, every temptation, and every harassment of the devil. The devil attacks our minds with fear and anxiety – if it were not for His Grace that overshadows you and me through every challenge, what would we do?

Sometimes His Grace seems like an invisible force field that stands between me and the destructive intentions of the devil. Sometimes His Grace seems like a cool glass of water on a very hot and humid day. Sometimes Grace resembles shooting me out like an arrow over every obstacle with the purpose of hitting God's intended target. In other words, the Grace of God is constantly with me.

How does the Grace of God help me with **Assimilation**? What am I absorbing with Grace? I absorb the idea that grace is for me. I embrace grace and absorb it in my very life. I don't receive the wrath of God for my sins; through His Grace, I receive and absorb His mercy, His love, His forgiveness, His confidence, and His peace. My confidence that God's Grace is continuously with me lets me know that I can do all things through Christ who gives me the strength to overcome.

With His Grace, I have the power to **Excrete** the very things that would limit me from following Christ to my fullest. His Grace gives me the help I need to eliminate fear and replace it with faith, to eliminate stagnation in my life and replace it with movement towards the purpose of God, to eliminate unforgiveness and live my life with forgiveness and freedom. His Grace gives me the spiritual shot in the arm I need to get rid of everything that could limit and stand in the way of my access to the promises of God.

His Grace gives me the strength to be an overcomer with **Adaptability**. Remember, Adaptability is characterized by how you respond to stress and trouble. In 2 Corinthians 12:7-9, when the Apostle Paul was in distress, God reassured him by saying that His Grace was more than enough to see him through and bring him through. As a result, the Apostle Paul was able to continue his godly assignment as an overcomer through the Grace of God. God's Grace allowed Paul to adapt to adversity without giving up or giving in to it. Through adaptability, His Grace gives me the confidence and strength to be flexible, versatile, skillful, resourceful, as well as free of worry and fear.

Because His Grace is with me, I can spiritually **Grow** and mature with excellence and grace. I have the capacity through His Grace to mature by going from glory to glory, from faith to faith. He gives me, with His Grace, the strength and confidence to complete the assignment that He has given me to do on this earth. His Grace nourishes me as I yield to Him and draw closer to Him, as I get to know Him intimately and mature in Him by giving Him glory in my life.

> *"But continue to grow and increase in God's grace and intimacy with our Lord and Savior, Jesus Christ. May he receive all the glory both now and until the day eternity begins. Amen!" (2 Peter 3:18 TPT)*

Reproduction is the ability to produce offspring as well as to replace an old life with a new life in Christ. I reproduce in others what God has given me, so when I reproduce grace, I not only give grace to others because I've been given grace, but I encourage others to walk in His Grace.

As we strive to spiritually mature in Him, let us remember His Grace, which is a constant reminder of God's love, mercy, and power upon us to do the impossible and live the possible life that He has promised us.

MUSING: THOUGHTS TO PROVOKE

"The proof of spiritual maturity is not how pure you are but awareness of your impurity. That very awareness opens the door to grace." – Philip Yancey

"Grace is the voice that calls us to change and then gives us the power to pull it off."– Max Lucado

QUESTIONS TO PONDER:

How has God shown you His grace as you mature? Think of some examples of how God has brought you through situations by His grace. What did you learn?

CHAPTER 7:
OUR HELP COMES FROM THE LORD – THE FIVE GRACES

So now, Beloved Ones, throughout this book we have worked to understand that in order to successfully fulfil the purpose of God, we must "grow up and grow deep" in Him. After we come to Christ we are not to stay the same but we are to go from glory to glory from faith to faith. We are not to play the church but be the church! Let's allow the brilliance that's in Him, shine through us. If we are to make disciples as Jesus commissioned, then we must spiritually mature so that we may become progenitors.

Our journey to spiritual maturity, as Manifested Sons and Daughters of God, is designed by Him for His pleasure because as we become more and more like Jesus Christ, our life gives Him glory. As we read and absorb God's Word, it washes, cleanses, and purifies us. As we fully partner with the Holy Spirit, we experience the transforming work inside of us that spills to the outside of us and positively and powerfully affects those within our sphere of influence. His Grace gives us the strength and confidence to become victorious against sin and unrighteousness. When we listen to the Progenitors and the 5 Fold Ministry that God has given to assist us in our spiritual maturation we flourish. Jesus wants to present to His Father mature Believers. But we have to do the work of spiritually growing to make sure we are in proper alignment to His will so that our life will give Him praise and glory.

> *"All that he does in us is designed to make us a mature church for his pleasure, until we become a source of praise to him—glorious and radiant, beautiful and holy, without fault or flaw." Ephesians 5:27 TPT*

When we come in proper alignment to His will, we become productive and fruitful.

> *"But blessed are those who trust in the Lord and have made the Lord their hope and confidence. They are like trees planted along a riverbank, with roots that reach deep into the water. Such trees are not bothered by the heat or worried by long months of drought. Their leaves stay green, and they never stop producing fruit." (Jeremiah 17:7,8 NLT)*

Again, so, let's be determined to grow up and grow deep in Him so that the fruit we produce can be lasting and perpetual. Remember, it's not an easy task and it takes time and energy. But if you love God with all of your heart, soul, mind, and strength, and you appreciate and value what Jesus did on Calvary, you'll want to run this purposeful race that God has set before you. It's not by your own strength and intellect that you fulfill this. Don't focus on the past but look towards the finish line. Remember, if one looks behind them while running a race, it has a tendency to slow them down. You don't need to focus on the distractions that come your way. But, finish well and finish strong by having that strong inward desire to complete the race. Be determined to not quit because of the challenges you're faced with. But, if you allow yourself to get excited about where God is taking you, persevere through adversity, and stay in the race, you will reach all that God has in store for you, the prize of victory!

> *"I admit that I haven't yet acquired the absolute fullness that I'm pursuing, but I run with passion into his abundance so that I may reach the purpose that Jesus Christ has called me to fulfill and wants me to discover. I don't depend on my own strength to accomplish this; however I do have one compelling focus: I forget all of the past as I fasten my heart to the future instead. I run straight for the divine invitation of reaching the heavenly goal and gaining the victory-prize through the anointing of Jesus." (Philippians 3:12-14 TPT)*

TAKEAWAYS

1. Spiritual growth is not a sprint, it's a marathon! Spiritual growth and maturation is not a matter of running or moving as fast as you can for a short distance to reach your goal. It takes endurance and faith to run this race and finish strong.

2. Be determined to finish strong in the Lord and the Power of His might.

3. Celebrate every victory, whether small or large.

4. A mature person takes responsibility for their actions and doesn't kid themself.

5. Know that it's not easy, but it is doable.

6. A person who is maturing does a continuous self-reflection/self-assessment through the leading of the Holy Spirit to determine if there is anything that they need to change.

7. It is important to adjust ourselves quickly to change.

8. Maturity allows us to discern good from evil without relying on our emotions and our will to determine it.

9. Our lives need to reflect His glory. When He created Adam and Eve, He created them to reflect His glory on the earth so that the earth would be filled with His fullness and His grace.

10. The more we grow and mature, the more of God's glory shows through us, and the brighter the light of His glory shines from us!

11. Rely on the five Graces that God has given us to help us grow: The Holy Spirit, The Word of God, Five-Fold Ministry, Progenitors, and His Grace.

12. Determine your motivation for authentic spiritual growth.

13. Stay focused on your goals, your God-given purpose, and your God-given assignment.

14. Yield your will to the will of God and your mind to the mind of Christ.

15. Always remember to repent and ask God for forgiveness, because He's faithful and just to forgive and cleanse.

16. Continuously pray in tongues, your spiritual language.

17. Put on and keep on the whole armor of God (Ephesians 6).

18. Don't be afraid of the devil and his works – you have been given power of God to be more than a conqueror.

19. Know that the devil is always tempting you to keep you from the purposes of God, but you have the authority to resist him. Be always vigilant!

20. 20. Don't cooperate with the enemy of your soul by giving in to and rehearsing hurts, because that can lead to bitterness, which leads to self-defeat.

21. Your life is defined by the love and purposes of God.

22. Don't make the mistake of comparing yourself to others, but look to Jesus, who is the author and finisher of our faith.

23. Respond to the Word of God and the Holy Spirit as they illuminate the areas in our lives that need to change.

24. Keep a posture of humility and repentance.

25. Make that change and be that change!

26. The more you mature, the more you reflect the image of your Father God!

27. Develop a plan and strategy for growth.

28. You can win the war of the flesh against the spirit as long as you fight with the sword of the spirit, which is the Word of God!

29. Speak in tongues daily, hourly to build up the inner man.

30. Let your brilliance shine.

31. Stay humble.

32. If you have a problem, run to the throne not to the phone

> *"I pray with great faith for you, because I'm fully convinced that the One who began this glorious work in you will faithfully continue the process of maturing you and will put his finishing touches to it until the unveiling of our Lord Jesus Christ!" (Philippians 1:6 TPT)*

ONWARDS & UPWARDS IN JESUS' NAME!

"Now, may the grace and joyous favor of the Lord Jesus Christ, the unambiguous love of God, and the precious communion that we share in the Holy Spirit be yours continually. Amen" (2 Corinthians 13:14)

BLESSINGS!

BIBLIOGRAPHY

Adams, Jay E. 2009. *Competent to Counsel: Introduction to Nouthetic Counseling.*

Anthony, Michelle. "Social Development in 3-5 Year Olds." https://www.scholastic.com/parents/family-life/social-emotional-learning/development-milestones/social-development-3-5-year-olds.html

Bible.org

Covey, Stephen R. 1989. *The 7 Habits of Highly Effective People: Powerful Lessons in Personal Change.*

Dicker, Rachel. 2016. "During Conception, Human Eggs Emit Sparks." https://www.usnews.com/news/articles/2016-04-26/human-eggs-emit-zinc-sparks-at-moment-of-fertilization

Dictionary.com

DuPont, Tianna. 2012. "Seed and Seedling Biology." https://extension.psu.edu/seed-and-seedling-biology

Fowler, James M. 1995. Stages of Faith: *The Psychology of Human Development and the Quest for Meaning.*

FreeChristianIllustrations.com

Khaliq, Ariba. 2011. "Emotional Development in Children 7-12 Years." https://www.onlymyhealth.com/emotional-development-in-children-years-1304405385

MacArthur, John. 2014. "Who Is Responsible For Your Spiritual Growth?" https://www.gty.org/library/blog/B140707/who-is-responsible-for-your-spiritual-growth

161

McLeod, Saul. 2018. "Erik Erikson's Stages of Psychosocial Development." https://www.simplypsychology.org/Erik-Erikson.html

Morris, Leon. "Justification." https://www.biblestudytools.com/dictionary/justification/

New American Standard New Testament Greek Lexicon. https://www.biblestudytools.com/lexicons/greek/nas/

Rogers, Adrian. "The Battle of the Mind." https://www.oneplace.com/ministries/love-worth-finding/read/articles/battle-of-the-mind-9743.html

Seattle Christian Counseling. 2014. "Inside Passive-Aggression: A Christian Counselor's Thoughts." https://seattlechristiancounseling.com/articles/inside-passive-aggression-a-christian-counselors-thoughts-2

"Stagnation." *Merriam-Webster.com Dictionary*, Merriam-Webster, https://www.merriam-webster.com/dictionary/stagnation. Accessed 13 Apr. 2020.

Steinfeld, Mary Beth. 2010. "Bonding is essential for normal infant development." https://health.ucdavis.edu/medicalcenter/healthtips/20100114_infant-bonding.html

Strong, James, 2007. Strong's Exhausted Concordance of the Bible. Updated and Expanded Edition.

Swanson, James A. 1997. *Dictionary of Biblical Languages with Semantic Domains: Greek New Testament*.

WordHippo.com

Thomas, W. LaVerne. 2010. *Sociology: The Study of Human Relationships*.

Traster, Tina. 2014. "A Story of Adoption and Reactive Attachment Disorder." https://www.psychologytoday.com/ie/blog/against-all-odds/201405/story-adoption-and-reactive-attachment-disorder

Vine, W.E., Merrill Unger, and William White Jr. 1996. V*ine's Complete Expository Dictionary of Old and New Testament Words*.

www.ingramcontent.com/pod-product-compliance
Lightning Source LLC
Chambersburg PA
CBHW071714090426
42738CB00009B/1766